The Craft Heritage Trails of Western North Carolina

Authors
Jay Fields and Brad Campbell

Designer
Mark Wilson

Project Coordinator
Robin Daniel

Published by HandMade in America, Inc.
67 North Market Street, Asheville, North Carolina 28802
(704) 252-0121
http://www.haywood.cc.nc.us/wncedc

Acknowledgments

This guidebook was developed under the auspices of HandMade in America, an organization dedicated to the nurturance of craft culture and community in Western North Carolina. Research, creative development and first printing of the guidebook has been funded with grants from the Pew Partnership for Civic Change, the North Carolina Division of Travel and Tourism, the Federal Highway Administration, the Tennessee Valley Authority, and Advantage West. The North Carolina Department of Transportation, Scenic Highways Division, aided in the coordination of ISTEA (Intermodal Surface Transportation Efficiency Act) federal grant assistance.

In addition to the working committees and board of HandMade in America, other Western North Carolina associations aided in the composition of both the loop tours and the guidebook itself. Those groups include three regional tourism organizations: Blue Ridge Host, High Country Host, and Smoky Mountain Host. The editors also gratefully acknowledge heritage tourism committees throughout the trails area for assistance in submitting prospective sites for inclusion in the loop system and the National Trust for Historic Preservation for its generous support.

HAND MADE
in
AMERICA

HandMade in America

ADVANTAGEWEST
NORTH CAROLINA

Table of Contents

This is more than a simple guidebook to craft. It is the story of people. People whose lives are colored by their art and whose art colors the lives of anyone who comes to know their work. And where are these people? They're "down the road a piece" or "round the bend" or "within shoutin' distance." And they're in this book. Consider, for example, the following:

Under the roof of a 100-year-old chestnut barn somewhere outside Sylva, a young woman patiently coaxes a human form out of a block of marble in the method of a Renaissance master. 🖐 *In the shadow of the Smokies, a Cherokee woman weaves river cane into a basket using movements that belong not only to her, but to an ancestry that predates our country.*

🖐 *At the edge of the Penland campus, a former rocket*

scientist experiments with new dinnerware glazes in his basement studio. ✋ *On looms that have shuttled for decades, women of the Crossnore community make woven goods prized by presidents and favorite uncles.* ✋ *Not far from Brevard, hundreds of summer campers get up to their elbows in wet clay under the joyous guidance of a kindred spirit.* ✋ *And near John C. Campbell Folk School in Brasstown, a slender, friendly gentlemen shows guests his work—gouged-out bowls and platters made from trees he planted as seedlings.* ✋ This book is an invitation. It invites you to discover a world you may have no idea existed. Because here in the mountains and hill country of Western North Carolina, where you can see only as far as the next bend, something of timeless grace unfolds.

fYI

**Helpful
Stuff
To Know**

**CELEBRATING THE
ROAD LESS
TRAVELED.**

**Throughout the
state, there are
thirty-one scenic
byways, designated
and maintained by
the North Carolina
Department of
Transportation.
These roads offer
something more
than a simple route
from one point to
another. They lead
you past shifting
landscapes of natural
beauty and wonder.**

**Panoramic vistas
give way to intimate
drives under the
canopies of
evergreen forests
and just as quickly
open up again to the
sight of distant
mountains.
Whitewater rivers
and quiet streams
sidle up alongside for
a mile or two and
then wander off.   >**

HOW TO USE THIS GUIDEBOOK

We've detailed seven driving loops of varying lengths, with almost 400 stops listed. There is no set time for discovering the crafts and attractions on a single trail. Depending on the time you have to invest, you can bite off all or a part of any loop.

For each trail a map shows the location and category of the stops. Listings are numbered sequentially based on a starting point and routing that seemed most natural to the editors. However, feel free to pick up the loop at any point and go in any direction you please. You may even wish to combine parts of two adjoining loops. A North Carolina State Map, available by calling the N.C. Division of Travel and Tourism (919-733-7600 in state, 800-847-4862 out of state) is a nice item to have handy for jumping from one trail to the next, and complements the maps provided.

In addition to the specific trails, which in most cases are actual loops, there are "spurs" indicated that strike out in one direction from the loop to capture a destination or scenic highway of high interest. We encourage you to include these excursions as part of your overall tour.

PLANNING YOUR TRIP

To enrich your experience, we suggest that you:

Come ready to enjoy yourself

According to your interest, sample some of the book offerings listed in this guide prior to setting out.

Go with the flow

The mountains have a rhythm and a pace of their own. The more slowly you go, the richer the experience. Here's a rule to go by: Determine how long it normally takes you to do something. Then double it.

Learn about the maker

The real treasure is often the story behind the piece. Ask questions. Crafts work is close to the heart; people like to talk about it. On the other hand, it's good to remember that craftspeople's time is often precious. Please respect posted hours for studios listed in this book.

Strike out on your own

If you see an interesting road that's off the map, take it. Getting lost (and found again) is half the fun.

Patchwork fields and hillsides stretch to the horizon, sown with colors of the season.

Wherever practical, our trails overlay these N.C. Scenic Byways routes. Of the eleven byways located in western North Carolina, ten of them are on or near one of the Craft Heritage Trails. The byways are clearly indicated on the individual loop maps and described in the accompanying section of text. When you're on the road, they're marked by the sign above.

There are many treasures out there waiting for you on the Craft Heritage Trails of W.N.C. We hope you find one of them to be the journey itself.

FYI

Helpful Stuff To Know

STUFF THE KNAPSACK (OR TRUNK)
How about: binoculars; *Peterson Field Guides* to birds, trees, and wild flowers; extra sweater; shoes to wade in; copy of *War and Peace* (unabridged) for pressing dried flowers; four leaf clovers and other treasures; compass; a tin of Altoids (or other mints); flashlight; pocket-knife for slicing apples and spreading peanut butter for sandwiches on the run; a blanket for naps on sunny hillsides or star gazing on mountain tops; reading glasses; sun screen; floppy hat and walkingstick.

And be sure to bring your checkbook (many studios and some stores are not set up for credit cards.)

Record your good times

Whether you choose a notebook, sketch pad, camera or watercolors, recording your journey will allow you to revisit your experiences.

Call ahead about special needs

If you or someone in your party has physical restrictions and needs special assistance, we strongly suggest you call ahead. Many studios are in private homes so handicap access varies considerably

LISTING CRITERIA

Individual committees and host groups within the 21-county region submitted sites for consideration. The editors used the following criteria:

- *Studios that offer dependable times for guests to visit.*
- *Galleries that primarily carry objects made in the U.S.A., with a focus on North Carolina.*
- *Restaurants with a reputation for fine food and featuring dishes indigenous to the region.*
- *Inns and bed and breakfasts with a historical underpinning and an architecture that, in and of itself, bespeaks craft.*

FYI

**Helpful
Stuff
To Know**

We double-checked each site against these criteria and, in most cases, visited personally to capture a sense of each place. We know that sites on these trails will continue to evolve. This is the first edition of a volume HandMade hopes to publish, with updates, over many years. Telephone numbers, addresses, and other information contained within is accurate, to the best of our knowledge, as of the date of publication. We know there are other studios, galleries, restaurants, and inns in the region that qualify for a listing in this directory. For those we missed in this initial volume, we apologize and urge you to ask for a listing in subsequent editions.

TO FIND EVEN MORE STUDIOS
We encourage you to inquire further at galleries and information centers about those craft demonstration sites and studios that are open on a "by appointment" basis and, for that reason, not included in this book. Another good starting place for finding these other craftspeople is the directory of local chambers of commerce and host group organizations on the following pages.

HELPFUL PHONE NUMBERS
Host Groups
Blue Ridge Host
(Polk, Rutherford, McDowell, Yancey, Buncombe, Transylvania, Henderson and Madison Counties)
(800) 807-3391

High Country Host
(Mitchell, Alleghany, Ashe, Avery, and Watauga Counties)
(704) 264-1299
(800) 438-7500

There's a great tradition of music in these mountains. Here is just a sampling of places where you can catch our talented local artists live on stage:

Asheville

Alternative Pub
  (704) 254-7475
Barley's Brew Pub
  (704) 255-0504
Be Here Now
  (704) 258-2071
Bean Streets
  (704) 255-8180
The Bier Garden
  (704) 285-0002
Gatsbys
  (704) 254-4248
Karmasonics
  (704) 259-9949
Malaprops
  (704) 254-6734
31 Patton
  (704) 254-5731

Black Mountain

Gray Eagle
  (704) 669-8734
Town Pump
  (704) 669-9151

Blowing Rock

Twigs
  (704) 295-5050 >

Smoky Mountain Host

(Jackson, Graham, Clay, Swain, Cherokee, Macon, and Haywood Counties)

(800) 432-4678
(704) 369-9606

Chambers of Commerce & Visitors Centers

Andrews	(704) 321-3584
Ashe County (West Jefferson)	(910) 246-9550
Asheville	(704) 258-6111
	(800) 257-1300
Avery County (Newland)	(704) 733-4737
Black Mountain	(704) 669-2300
	(800) 669-2301
Beech Mountain	(704) 387-2983
	(800) 468-5506
Boone	(800) 852-9506
	(704) 264-2225
Brevard/Transylvania County	(704) 883-3700
	(800) 648-4523
Burke County (Morganton)	(704) 437-3021
Cashiers Area	(704) 743-5191
Cherokee Visitors Center	(800) 438-1601
	(704) 497-9195
Clay County (Hayesville)	(704) 389-3704
Cleveland County (Shelby)	(704) 487-8521
Franklin	(800) 336-7829

	(704) 524-3161
Graham County	
(Robbinsville)	(704) 479-3790
	(800) 470-3790
Haywood County	
(Waynesville)	(800) 334-9036
Greater Hendersonville	(704) 692-1413
Highlands	(704) 526-2112
Jackson County	
(Sylva)	(704) 586-2155
	(800) 962-1911
Madison County	
(Mars Hill)	(704) 689-9351
Maggie Valley	(800) 624-4431
McDowell County	
(Marion)	(704) 652-4240
	(800) 227-3912
Mitchell County	
(Spruce Pine)	(704) 765-9483
Rutherford County	
(Rutherfordton)	(704) 287-3090
Swain County	
(Bryson City)	(800) 867-9246
(704) 488-3681	
Tryon-Thermal Belt	(704) 859-6236
Wilkes County	(910) 838-8662
Yancey County	
(Burnsville)	(704) 682-7413
	(800) 948-1632

Emergency Numbers

N.C. Highway Patrol

Asheville Communication	
Centers	(800) 445-1772
Cellular phones	*47 (Toll free)

Boone
The Blues
(704) 898-8988
Carribean Cafe
(704) 265-2233
The Klondike Cafe
(704) 262-5065

Brevard
Falls Landing
(704) 884-2835

Bryson City
The Welkin
(704) 488-2300

Celo
Celo Inn
(704) 675-5132

Sylva
City Lights Cafe
(704) 586-9499

Morganton
Comma
(704) 433-SHOW

Rutherfordton
Rutherford Towne
Beanery
(704) 286-0187

Valdese
Old Rock School
(704) 879-2129

Hickory
Drips Coffee Shop
(704) 324-1644
Fireman's Kitchen
(704) 324-5951

FYI

Helpful Stuff To Know

OLD TIMEY MUSIC
There's a musical tradition here that's also handmade. It originated in Ireland, Scotland and England and was brought here by early settlers. This tradition continues today, kept alive by many fine musicians like these:

Sheila Kay Adams
Singer, storyteller
Mars Hill, NC

Laura Boosinger
Banjo player, singer
Asheville, NC

Arvil Freeman
Fiddler
Weaverville, NC

Bruce Green
Fiddler
Bursnville, NC

David Holt
Multi-instrumentalist, singer, storyteller
Asheville, NC

Don Pedi
Lap dulcimer player
Grapevine, NC

Luke Smathers
Fiddler
Canton, NC

Doug Wallin
Ballad singer
Marshall, NC

Doc Watson
Singer, Guitar player
Deep Gap, NC

RECOMMENDED READING

Garry G. Barker, *The Handcraft Revival in Southern Appalachia, 1930-1990.* Knoxville: The University of Tennessee Press, 1991.

Blue Ridge Mountains Guidebooks, Inns of the Blue Ridge, Mountain Hospitality in the Best Southern Tradition from Virginia to Georgia. McLean Virginia: EMP Publication, Inc. 1993.

LeGuette Blythe, ed., *Gift Of The Hills: Miss Lucy Morgan's Story Of Her Unique Penland School.* Chapel Hill: University of North Carolina Press, 1958, 1971.

Fred Chappell, *I Am One Of You Forever.* Baton Rouge: Louisiana State University Press, 1985.

Wilma Dykeman, *The French Broad.* Newport, Tennessee: Wakestone Books, 1992.

Allen H. Eaton, *Handcrafts of the Southern Highlands.* New York: Dover Publications, Inc., 1937, 1973. (Supported and originally published by Russell Sage Foundation.)

John Ehle, *The Journey of August King.* Hyperion Paperback, 1995.

Helpful Stuff To Know

Janet Fitch, *The Art and Craft of Jewelry*. San Francisco: Chronicle Books, 1994.

Frances Louisa Goodrich, with a new introduction by Jan Davidson. *Mountain Homespun*. Knoxville: The University of Tennessee Press, 1989. A facsimile of the original published in 1931.

Suzanne W. Jones, *Growing Up in the South, An Anthology of Modern Southern Literature*, Mentor Book, 1991.

Sara Pacher and Linda Davis March, *The Insiders Guide To North Carolina's Mountains*. Charlotte: Knight Publishing Company, 1995.

Carolyn Sakowski, *Touring the Western North Carolina Backroads*. Winston-Salem: John F. Blair Publisher, 1990.

Charlotte F. Speight and John Toki, *Hands In Clay, An Introduction To Ceramics*. Mountain View, CA: Mayfield Publishing, 1995.

Tova Martin, *Tasha Tudor's Heirloom Crafts*. Boston, New York: Houghton Mifflin, 1995

Thomas Wolfe, *Look Homeward, Angel*. New York: Chas. Scribner's, 1957.

A HIGHLY SUBJECTIVE LIST OF MUSIC FOR THE CAR Aaron Copeland's *Appalachian Spring*, anything by Bill Monroe or Doc Watson, *Grandfather's Greatest Hits* by David Holt, *Arkansas Traveler* by Michelle Shocked, anything by Vivaldi, Bach, or Marion McPartland; Alison Krauss & Union Station's *Every Time You Say Goodbye*, Jim Taylor's *Come Before Winter*, Bela Fleck, Mark O'Connor, Leo Kottke, and Asheville's own David Wilcox. Or just tune in either of the area's public radio stations, WCQS at 88.1 or WNCW at 88.7

A number of the galleries listed in this book offer a notable selection of music by our regional artists. It's worth the trouble to search them out.

High Country Ramble

The treasures of the High Country utterly refuse to confine themselves to one simple route or one tidy description. Rare finds, discoveries and must-sees branch off the main trail like the offshoots of a young evergreen. ☀ The ground over which you travel is just as varied as the discoveries you will make. Departing the Blue Ridge Parkway at Glendale Springs, you watch the mountains flatten out to a loose shrug. Or maybe it's just a trick of the eye: for here you are not dodging through hollows and coves, but skirting along above them on the crest of the Blue Ridge. It feels like you are traveling along the very rim of the earth. Farther on, the mountains deepen again, and you find yourself back in their folds. ☀ Whether you are on top of the mountains or among them, prepare for surprises. In Glendale Springs and West Jefferson you will see religious frescoes of such beauty that they could have been created centuries ago for a great European cathedral. In Linville, homes and churches designed by one of the great architects of this century, Francis

The faces of these mountains by wood carver Tom Wolfe.

Along the Rim of the Earth

Bacon, are clad in chestnut bark. And in Todd and Valle Crucis, turn-of-the-century general stores look and feel as though they've been frozen in time. ☀ In Boone and Blowing Rock and Foscoe you will come across an unrivaled collection of galleries that feature traditional and contemporary work from the hands of craftspeople scattered all throughout the high country. Some of these crafters are newcomers. Others have been here their whole lives. But all of them have found in these high places the right mixture of solitude and community that fuels inspiration. ☀ And finally, in Crossnore, you will have a chance to see how a small clutch of weavers, armed with nothing but simple looms, produces miracles for mountain children. ☀ All of this and much more are out there waiting for you on the High Country Ramble. To uncover all that this journey has to offer, bring along your sense of adventure. Follow the trail. Take the side trips. Then strike out on your own. And remember: on a ramble, there are no rules. And no wrong turns.

High Country Ramble

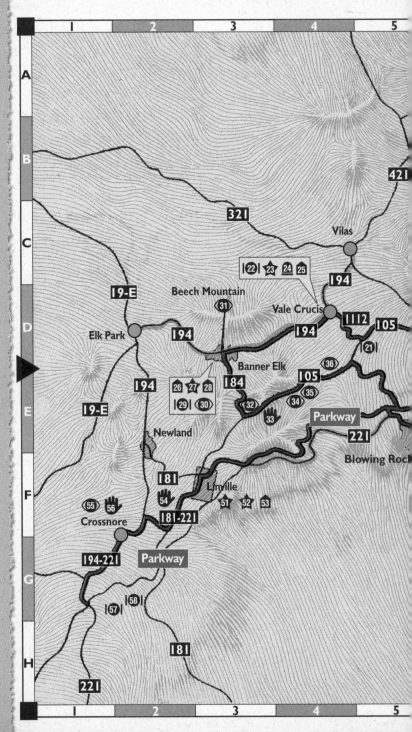

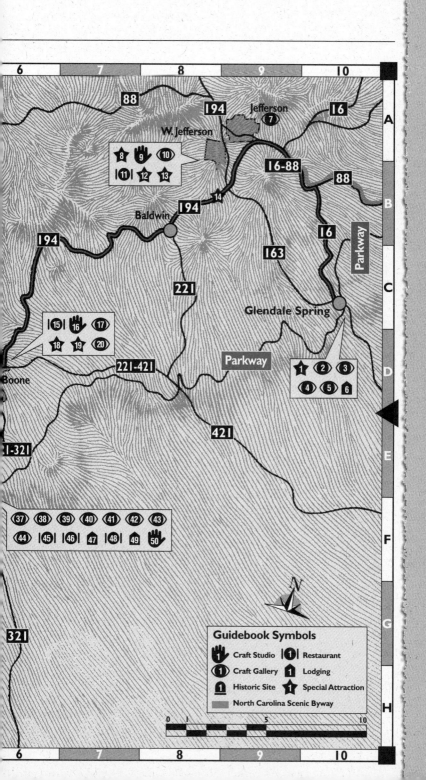

19

6   7   8   9   10

88

194

Jefferson
7

W. Jefferson

A

★8 ✋9 ⑩
⑪ 12 13

16

16-88

88

194

14

16

Baldwin

B

Parkway

194

221

163

C

⎮15 ✋16 ⑰
18 19 ⑳

Glendale Spring

Boone

221-421

Parkway

★1 ②③
④⑤6

D

421

I-321

E

⑨37 ⑨38 ⑨39 ⑨40 ⑨41 ⑨42 ⑨43
⑨44 ⎮45 ⎮46 47 ⎮48 49 ✋50

F

N

G

321

Guidebook Symbols

✋1 Craft Studio   ⎮1⎮ Restaurant

①1 Craft Gallery   1 Lodging

1 Historic Site   ★1 Special Attraction

  North Carolina Scenic Byway

0   1   5   10

H

6   7   8   9   10

High Country Ramble

Unquestionably a ramble, this loop meanders over some 120 miles, easily a two to three day adventure.

Exit the Blue Ridge Parkway at Horse Gap (Milepost 259). Take Hwy 16 to the town of Glendale Springs.

Holy Trinity church in Glendale Springs.

GLENDALE SPRINGS

1 **Church of the Frescoe** HOLY TRINITY EPISCO-PAL CHURCH, HWY 16 AT GLENDALE SPRINGS. Four ecclesiastical frescoes. The largest work, "The Last Supper," is by Ben Long. The others were painted by his students. The technique, sensitivity, and beauty in these works is astonishing. Daily. No phone.

2 **Greenhouse Crafts Shop** 248 JOHN LUKE RD. Across the street from Holy Trinity in an old school house. A fine collection of Celtic music on tapes and CD's along with a mix of handmade items and curiosities. Seven days, 10–5. (910) 982-2618

3 **Silver Designs** 275 JOHN LUKE RD. Silver designs using natural gems and stones from these mountains. The hospitality of the owner is the genuine article; so is the work. Seven days, 10–6. (910) 982-4102

4 **Glendale Springs Glass and Clay Gallery** HWY 16. Husband and wife partners. 18th century pottery recreations; paperweights, functional and decorative blown glass; fine art photography. Seven days, 10–5. Closed Jan–April. (910) 982-3662

5 **Northwestern Trading Post** PARKWAY MILEPOST 259 AT GLENDALE SPRINGS. A non-profit emporium featuring crafts, antiques, souvenirs, and food (stack cakes out front). Seven days, 9–5:30, April 15–Oct 31. (910) 982-2543

6 **Glendale Springs Inn and Restaurant** HWY 16 AT GLENDALE SPRINGS. Owners Amanda and Larry Smith have given a thoughtful restoration to this inn, listed on the National Register of Historic Places. Wrap-around porch is the perfect place to wile away an afternoon or enjoy a Sunday brunch. (910) 982-2103 or (800) 287-1206

JEFFERSON

7 **Unique Illusions Gallery** MAIN ST. Whimsical hand-painted furniture and serious oil paintings. Incongruous pairing, but these two artists make it work, and wonderfully. Tues–Fri, 10–5; Sat, 10–3. (910) 246-2598

The Road Goes On Forever
Side Trips, adventures, and treasure hunts

OXYMORON, ANYONE?
The oldest river in America is the New River, whose north and south forks run through Watauga, Ashe and Alleghany counties.

WEST JEFFERSON

8 **Church of the Frescoe** ST. MARY'S EPISCOPAL CHURCH, BEAVER CREEK RD. Rev. J. Faulton Hodge invited painter Ben Long to adorn this simple church in the early 70's and inspire parishioners. Here you will see "Mary Great with Child," "John the Baptist," and "The Mystery of Faith." Daily. No phone.

9 **Tom Wolfe's Mountain Meadow Studio** 103 S. JEFFERSON AVE. You could learn a lot about woodcarving by studying Wolfe's imaginative work, or by reading one of the 30-some books he's authored on the subject. All kinds of critters carved from all kinds of woods. Buy the real thing or a reproduction. Mon–Sat, 9–5. (910) 246-9771

10 **Ashe Custom Framing & Gallery** 105 S. JEFFERSON AVE. More than you'd expect. A frame shop, but also a gallery of local pottery and other crafts. Tues–Fri, 10–5; Sat 10–2. (910) 246-2218

11 **Greenfield Campground and Restaurant** HWY 163, ONE AND A HALF MILES FROM TOWN. Picture postcard views served up with country-style ham, pan-fried chicken, red-eye gravy, mountain trout, homemade biscuits, and fried apple pie. Breakfast, lunch and dinner. Daily. (910) 246-5177

The work of Tom Wolfe, up close and personal.

Other West Jefferson Attractions

12 **Ashe County Cheese** MAIN & FOURTH AVE. "The Carolinas' only cheese manufacturer." Mon–Sat, 8–5. (919) 246-2501

13 **Ashe County Arts Council** FOURTH AVE. A renovated WPA building from the 1930s with periodic craft exhibits.

Of Note, Off The Loop

Shatley Springs Restaurant HWY 16 TO SHATLEY SPRINGS ROAD, CRUMPLER. People once came from far and wide to bathe in the healing waters of the nearby spring. Today they flock here for belt-loosening meals created and served up the old-fashioned way. Bring your grandmother. She'll approve. Daily 7 am–9 pm (May–Oct). (910) 982-2236

River House Inn & Restaurant ON THE NORTH FORK OF THE NEW RIVER ON OLD FIELD CREEK ROAD OFF HWY 16 IN GRASSY CREEK. An historic inn and five star restaurant in a pristine riverside setting. Meal reservations suggested. (910) 982-2109.

A tip of the hat to the Todd General Store.

Guidebook Symbols

 Craft Studio   Restaurant

Craft Gallery   Lodging

Historic Site   Special Attraction

The regulars convene
out front at Todd
General Store.

TODD

14 **Todd General Store** 194 SOUTH OUT OF W.
JEFFERSON. TURN OFF 194 AT SIGN OF THE GOOSE.
A rumpled, but proud survivor. Load up on gro-
ceries, garden seeds, penny candy and dry goods.
Local news, wisdom and outright whoppers are
also plentiful as neighbors congregate on the front
porch or around the pot-bellied stove. It opened
in 1904, and the only thing that's changed is the
trains don't run anymore. In summer, Mon–Sat
7–7; Sun 12:30–5. In winter, Mon–Sat 8–6; Sun
12:30–5. (910) 877-1067

BOONE

15 **Dan'l Boone Inn** AT THE JUNCTION OF US 321
AND 421. Traditional mountain foods served in
abundance, one platter after another. Popular with
families across the street and across the country.
(704) 264-8657

16 **Doe River Pottery** 149 W. KING ST. After a meal
at Dan'l Boone, it's a pleasant three-block stroll
to this destination. Large studio and small gallery.
Even from the street, this colorful, distinctive pottery will catch your eye. Mon–Sat, 10–6; Sun, 1–6.
(704) 264-1127

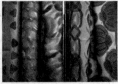

Laura Holshouser's
hand-dyed and hand-
painted silks.

17 **Hands Gallery** 454 KING ST, BOONE. One of the
area's oldest artist-owned galleries. The entire rep-
ertoire of craft, with a bent toward the softer
things, like silks and wovens. Mon–Sat 10–5; Sun,
12–4. (704) 262-1970

18 **Jones House** KING ST. Housing the Arts Council
Museum. Three-story, shingled Arts & Crafts house
on prominent perch. Exhibits vary. Wed–Sat, 1–5.
(704) 262-4576

19 **Appalachian Cultural Museum** UNIVERSITY
HALL, ON THE CAMPUS OF APPALACHIAN STATE
UNIVERSITY. Life in the mountains, from prehis-
tory forward, illuminated in a fine way for self-
directed or guided tours. Tues–Sat, 10–5; Sun, 1–5.
(704) 262-3117

20 **Artisans Gallery** 1711 HWY 105. A co-op with an
uncommonly high quality of work. Museum-like
displays of pottery and jewelry. Take note, especially, of the iridescent raku urns and fish. Mon–
Sat, 10–6; Sun, 12–6. (704) 265-0100

*Depart Boone on NC 105, turning right at blinker light onto Broadstone
toward Valle Crucis.*

The Road Goes On Forever

Side Trips, adventures,
and treasure hunts

TUNE IN TO YOUR LOCAL INSECT.
*The psychic powers of certain small mountain
creatures are held in such esteem that their human
friends have been known to honor them at important
social functions. Examples: Boone's Firefly Festival in
July and Banner Elk's Wooly Worm Festival in October.*

VALLE CRUCIS

21 **Ham Shop** CORNER OF BROADSTONE AND HWY 105. Famous for their ham biscuits. Other menu items include salads and soups. (704) 963-6310

22 **Mast Farm Inn** SR 1112 FROM HWY 105 TO VALLE CRUCIS. Time passes most agreeably on the expansive wraparound porch of this 18th century inn. As you wait for the dinner bell to ring, look for the two-story, log house built in 1812. It served as a loom house for Aunt Josie and Aunt Leona Mast, who wove linens for the White House of President Wilson. Reservations suggested for these bountiful, family-style meals. Tues–Sat, 6 and 7:45; Sun, 12:30 and 2:30. (704) 963-5857

23 **Mast General Store (the original) & Annex** SR 1112, VALLE CRUCIS. The tradition of the country store, gussied up. Purveyors of quality goods and miscellany since 1882. Folks have been known to get lost in here for weeks. Mon–Sat, 10–6; Sun, 1–6. (704) 963-6511

24 **Valle Crucis Episcopal Mission** NC 194, BETWEEN VALLE CRUCIS AND BANNER ELK. Quiet place high on the mountain. A stone church was

"Torso" by Richard Hallier

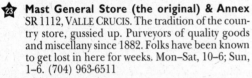

"Acrobags" by glass artists John Littleton and Kate Vogel.

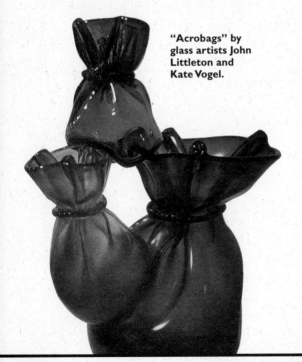

Guidebook Symbols

Craft Studio   Restaurant

Craft Gallery   Lodging

Historic Site   Special Attraction

Pottery by Pye in the Skye.

More thoughtful work by Rodney Shaw.

established in 1842 by the Right Rev. Levi Ives.

25 **River Valley Inn** WATAUGA RIVER ROAD. This inn is almost as old as our country. It was built in 1790 as a private residence. And it's no doubt just as secluded and peaceful as it was back then. Breakfast served to inn guests. (800) 297-3820

BANNER ELK

26 **Tufts House Inn** TWO MILES SOUTH OF BANNER ELK ON HWY 194, THEN RIGHT ONTO EDGAR TUFTS RD. FOR HALF MILE. Estate of the Tufts family, revered for development in Banner Elk, including Lees McRae College. Year-round. (704) 898-7944.

27 **Lees-McCrae College** CROSSROADS OF HWY 194 AND 184. Sixty-two buildings, many of native stone. At 4,000 ft., the highest college east of the Mississippi. Chartered in 1907, the school was an early provider of craft training. Work by blacksmith Daniel Boone is visible in door latches, hinges and light fixtures. Guided tours available through Registrar's Office during regular school terms.

28 **Banner Elk Bed & Breakfast** APPROXIMATELY HALF MILE NORTH OF BANNER ELK ON HWY 194. Once a church, now a raspberry-colored guest house. Year-round. (704) 898-6223

|29| **Beech Haus Restaurant** THROUGH BANNER ELK ON 194, TAKE HWY 184 TOWARD BEECH MOUNTAIN. Known for their fresh mountain trout, filleted at your table. Try the apple pan dowdy for dessert. Daily, 5–9. (704) 898-4246

30 **Sheer Bliss** 598 OLD TURNPIKE RD. NW. Gold and silver jewelry. Also gems, which neighborhood college students sometimes use to research class assignments. Mon–Sat, 10–5. (704) 898-9800

BEECH MOUNTAIN

31 **Works of Wood** HWY 184 ON TOP OF BEECH MOUNTAIN. Custom trunks, chests, tables and hutches made from a selection of fine woods. Seven days; 9:30–6:30. (704) 387-2373

HWY 105 BACK TOWARD BOONE

32 **Morning Star Gallery** AT TYNECASTLE, INTERSECTION OF HWYS 105 AND 184. Dimensional tapestries dramatize this artfully arrayed and beautifully chosen collection. Year-round. Mon–Sat, 10–5 (Summer). Mon–Sat, 12–5 (Winter). (704) 898-6047

The Road Goes On Forever

Side Trips, adventures, and treasure hunts

CHRISTMAS TREE CAPITAL OF THE WORLD.
Avery County is home to more growing Fraser firs than any other county in America. The tree was named after Scotsman John Fraser.

33 **Baskets D'Vine** HWY 105, FOSCOE. Traditional vine baskets and a nice collection of folk birdhouses. Mon–Sat, 10–5, closed Wed. (704) 963-6166

34 **The Potters Gallery at Creekside** HWY 105, FOSCOE. Just downstairs from Carlton Gallery. A stunning collection, simply displayed on weathered planks. Look for owner, Tim Turner, working at the wheel in his studio, located just behind the gallery space. Mon–Sat, 10–5; Sun 11–5. (704) 963-4258

35 **Carlton Gallery at Creekside** HWY 105, FOSCOE. From the parking lot, follow the winding footpath, cross over the bridge and the school of speckled trout, pass the leaping sculpture of a fish and a wading bird, and then climb a set of stairs to a wonderland of crafts and art. Mon–Sat, 10–5; Sun, 11–5. (704) 963-4288

36 **Miters Touch** HWY 105, SIX MILES SOUTH OF BOONE. What more perfect structure to hold heirloom quality wood furniture and cabinetry than a rustic log cabin? Here you'll find pieces you could literally build a room around, along with quite affordable keepsake boxes to hold wishes in. Mon–Thurs, 8–5; Fri 9–3; Sat, 11–3. (704) 963-4445

"The Love Bench," by Bob Doster greets visitors to Carlton Gallery.

On Hwy 105, head north from Miters Touch for .2 miles, turning right into Hound Ear's entranceway and onto Shull's Mill Rd. Follow Shull's Mill to the Parkway, turning north. The Moses Cone mansion will appear shortly on your right.

BLOWING ROCK

37 **Moses H. Cone Mansion** MOSES CONE MEMORIAL PARK, MILEPOST 294, BLUE RIDGE PARKWAY. Stately former residence of textile manufacturer Moses Cone. Today it's home to Guild Crafts, a retail establishment of the Southern Highland Craft Guild. Inspiring work inside; inspiring views outside. Daily, 9–5:30 (May–October). (704) 295-7938

Moses H. Cone Mansion.

Leaving the mansion, follow the Parkway north to its intersection with US 321, then follow 321 less than two miles into Blowing Rock proper.

38 **Expressions Gallery** MAIN ST., ACROSS FROM THE POST OFFICE. Significant guild gallery. Most members live and work in the surrounding area. Standouts include oversized pottery and handwoven garments. Sun–Thurs, 10–6; Fri–Sat, 10–9. (704) 295-7839

Guidebook Symbols

Craft Studio   Restaurant
Craft Gallery   Lodging
Historic Site   Special Attraction

Miters Touch in Foscoe.

(39) Starwood Gallery 1505 MAIN ST. Well-chosen selection of American crafts in a bustling storefront environment. Mon–Thurs, 10–6, Fri–Sat, 10–9, Sun 10–5 (June through Oct); Mon–Sat, 10–5, Sun, 11–5 (Nov through May). (704) 295-9229

(40) Appalachian Rustic Furnishings 1085 N. MAIN STREET. Twig furniture raised to a new level. Worthy of a rustic summer lodge or an East Side co-op. Simple elegance. (704) 295-9554

(41) Fovea SUNSET DRIVE. A small, elegant shop where resident goldsmith Ronald Tharp offers original designs in jewelry and hollow ware. Tues–Sat, 10–5. (704) 295-4705

(42) High Country Candles INSIDE THE HISTORIC MARTIN HOUSE ON MAIN ST. The candle as sculpture. Watch these intricate creations emerge layer upon layer from the wax vat. Mon–Sat, 10–6; Sun, 12–5 (closed Jan). (704) 295-9655

(43) The Dulcimer Shop MARTIN HOUSE, MAIN STREET. Fine handmade dulcimers. Patient, experienced proprietor will take the time to answer all your questions. Through the week, 10–5 (June–October). No phone.

Traditional herringbone weave by Bennie Martin.

The Road Goes On Forever

Side Trips, adventures, and treasure hunts

BROWN MOUNTAIN LIGHTS.
Yes, they're out there. Somewhere north of Morganton. Are they car lights? Restless spirits? Cherokee widows looking for fallen braves? An engineer in 1771 reported, "The mountain emits vapors that inflame," but the "swamp gas" theory has since been largely discarded.

(44) Gems by Gemini IN THE MARTIN HOUSE, MAIN ST. Custom-design 14-carat, gold jewelry, gems, and gifts. Seven Days. 9–6 (May–Sept.); 10–5 (Oct.–April). (704) 295-7700

|(45)| Dockside Ira's WONDERLAND TRAIL, OFF LAUREL. Eat salmon, tuna, grouper and other water-dwelling delectables under a covered deck in the woods. Don't pass up the cornbread or the yams. Seven nights, 5pm–9pm. In summer, a lunch seating is added, 11:30–2. (704) 295-4008

|(46)| Crippen's Restaurant and Inn 239 SUNSET DR. A bright, creative, tablecloth restaurant of culinary note with airy rooms above in a delightful makeover of the former Sunshine Inn. Year-round. (704) 295-3487

(47) The Inn At Ragged Garden SUNSET DR. A handsome and stalwart inn with bark siding and flagstone drive. April-December. (704) 295-9703

Upstairs at Miters Touch.

|(48)| The Farm House Restaurant US 321. A merry institution. Perched on the rim of an escarpment, this place serves up regional cuisine spiced with the joyous collaborations of singing waiters and waitresses. Villas available for overnighters. (704) 295-7361

(49) The Green Park Inn US 321. A wonderful survivor of the rambling, frame hotels of the 1880's, sitting at 4,200 feet on property from which three rivers find their source. Pearl Buck and Calvin Coolidge stayed here and so did John D. Rockefeller who, consistent with his style, tipped with dimes and searched for golf tees after striking blows on "golf links as green as Emerald Isle." Year-round. (704) 295-3143

(50) Rare Earth Pottery 330 FOREST DR., NEAR THE PARKWAY. Worth the trouble to call and ask for directions to this fine studio. Vibrant glazes that cross the color spectrum. A summer studio with a magnificent view. Mon–Sat, 10–5 (June–mid-October). (704) 265-7402

From Blowing Rock, motor along one of the Parkway's most spectacular stretches, crossing the Linn Cove Viaduct, an engineering wonder. Leave the Parkway at the Linville exit.

LINVILLE

(51) Grandfather Mountain ON HWY 221, TWO MILES FROM LINVILLE AND ONE MILE UP. Mountain animal habitats. The highest swinging footbridge in America. And some of the finest alpine hiking in the Southeast. Seven days, 8–7, (April–October);

All Saints church in Linville.

Guidebook Symbols

 Craft Studio |(1)| Restaurant

(1) Craft Gallery   (1) Lodging

(1) Historic Site   Special Attraction

8–5 (Nov–March). Ticket office closes hour and a half before Mountain. (800) 468-7325

52 **All Saints Episcopal Church** CAROLINA AVE., ONE BLOCK NORTH OF ESEEOLA LODGE, HWY 105. Commissioned in 1910 by Agnes MacRae Parsley. Twigs, logs and bark elevated by a master architect to inspirational levels. Architect Henry Bacon also designed the Lincoln Memorial. Open daily.

53 **Linville Cottage Inn** RUFFIN ROAD OFF HWY 181 IN LINVILLE. A cottage built three generations ago and still held by a member of that family. If you like antiques and the taste of garden herbs with your breakfast, this is your place. Year-round. (704) 733-6551

PINEOLA

54 **Martin Handicrafts** ON HWY 221, ACROSS LINVILLE RIVER BRIDGE, NEXT BUILDING ON RIGHT. Broommaker, chair repairer, basket maker. "Do it right or not it all" was what Martin's father told him as a youngster. Judging by the quality weaving found in the chair bottoms, he listened. Mon–Sat, 9–9. (704) 733-2874

CROSSNORE

55 **Holden's Arts & Crafts** U.S. 221, CROSSNORE. Twig furniture and vine baskets by local people who learned the craft from their parents. Mon–Sat, 8–4. (704) 733-4658

56 **The Weaving Room at Crossnore School** SIX MILES FROM LINVILLE ON HWY 221, LOOK FOR SIGNS. On the looms in this rock cottage, community women have woven pieces that have warmed mountain children and comforted statesmen. And they still do. Mon–Fri, 8:30–5; Sat, 9–4. (704) 733-4660

LINVILLE FALLS

57 **Spears B-B-Q & Grill** INTERSECTION OF US 221 AND NC 183. A place of divided loyalties. Some swear by the pork, chicken and ribs prepared in a smokehouse out back and simmered in Betty and David Huskins' famous barbecue sauce. Others remain loyal to the mountain trout, the country ham, and the vegetables served Southern Appalachian style. You'll be in one camp or the other before you leave. Seven days, 11am–9pm (mid-May–Oct); Fri, 5pm–9pm, Sat, 11–9, Sun, 11–7 (Nov–mid-May). (704) 765-2658

The Road Goes On Forever
Side Trips, adventures, and treasure hunts

When the original Crossnore weaving house burned in 1935, 120 school kids formed a human chain, bringing river rock out of the cold stream to build the house you see today.

58 **Louise's Famous Rock House** US 221 AND NC 183. Outlaws steer clear. This is a popular stop for state troopers. The daily specials keep the troopers and law-abiding citizens well satisfied. But on Fridays and Saturdays, when they start throwing ribeyes on the outside grill, even the bad guys can't stay away. Breakfast, lunch, dinner. Seven days. Mon–Thurs, 6–7:30; Fri–Sat, 6–8; Sun, 6–7. (704) 765-2702

Other Inns in Boone and Blowing Rock

Grandma Jean's Bed & Breakfast BOONE. (704) 262-3670

Lion's Den Bed & Breakfast BOONE. (704) 963-5785

Gideon Ridge Inn, Bed & Breakfast BLOWING ROCK. (704) 295-3644

Maple Lodge Bed & Breakfast BLOWING ROCK. (704) 295-3331

Stone Pillar Bed & Breakfast BLOWING ROCK. (704) 295-4141

The Gamekeeper Restaurant and Inn BLOWING ROCK. (704) 963-7400

Even the birds get a place to sit at Martin's

**New River Valley
Little Parkway
Mission Crossing**

Two scenic byways overlay the High Country Trail. A third, Little Parkway, is nearby and is heartily recommended.

Between Baldwin and Boone on NC 194, the New River Valley Byway follows the path of the "Old Buffalo Trail," where these once-numerous beasts moved the ground. Along its 18 mile length, you'll be treated to rolling farm country landscapes framed by distant mountains.

Mission Crossing takes you between Vilas and Elk Park via narrow and curvy NC 194. Recreational vehicles and buses are not recommended for this route, which sidles back and forth along the northern range of the Roan Mountains.

Little Parkway, largely paralleling the Blue Ridge Parkway, is a touring delight. Located between Linville and Blowing Rock on US 221, this side trip unlocks seventeen miles of rushing creeks, dense evergreens and roadside stands aglow with jars of honey and cider.

 SPOT IT! It's somewhere on this loop. Can you find it?

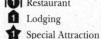

Guidebook Symbols

Craft Studio   Restaurant
Craft Gallery   Lodging
Historic Site   Special Attraction

Blue Ridge Parkway

The First Rural Parkway in the US.

A common thread cinches together the pearl-like trails of the craft heritage system. It drifts across ridge tops, tumbles into fertile river valleys, and zips back up to panoramic heights with natural grace. It brushes against waterfalls, rhododendron hells, and ancient mountainsides. And its very name – the Blue Ridge Parkway –

Wildcat Rocks overlook, 1947.

conjures up a certain Jack-Kerouac-Charles-Kuralt-all-American-romance-with-the-open-road-sort-of-thing.

There could hardly be a more fitting entranceway to the treasures of craft in these mountains.

Traveling south from Virginia, the Parkway follows the Blue Ridge, eastern rampart of the Appalachian mountains. It passes Mt. Mitchell, highest peak east of the Missssippi (6,684 feet), where you will skirt the southern end of the brooding Black Mountains, named for their dark green cloak of spruce and fir. From there, the road goes on to dodge and feint through the Craggies, the Pisgahs, the Balsams and the Great Smokies.

Pedestrian overlook at Fox Hunter's Paradise, 1940.

As you travel along this engineering masterpiece, keep in mind that the designers not only wished to create a road, but an illusion — the sense that each and every panorama along its entire length is part of one magnificent park.

Keep in mind, too, that the road is physical evidence of one of the great public works

Top: Elk Mountain parking overlook, 1953.
Bottom: Mahogany Rock, 1953.

projects of the century, manned by the Civil Conservation Corp, which Franklin Roosevelt established in the early 1930's to help put Americans back to work during the Great Depression.

And, finally, don't forget to ease off the accelerator. This is one road that's a destination in and of itself.

PHOTOS COURTESY OF BLUE RIDGE PARKWAY MUSEUM COLLECTION

Tunnel Construction, 1955.

Circle The Mountain

The "Circle The Mountain" driving tour is rich in diversity, crossing a century of rural life as easily as it slices through tobacco fields or plunges down hillsides of mountain laurel and rhododendron. ◉ Early on, you will drive through farmland and hamlets where craft developed as a pure necessity of life. Some of these farm communities and villages evoke a time when the mountains were largely cut off from the outside world. ◉ Quilts, hooked rugs, handkerchief dolls, whittled pieces, iron tools, vine baskets, and musical instruments. These became the art forged of the hard life of the mountains. ◉ The road over Doggett Mountain, a tumble of switchbacks, leads you into this earlier time. Watch for farm country where tobacco is harvested and cured in vented barns. Where a rock school house, now abandoned, stubbornly holds a piece of history that refuses to yield to modern contrivance. Where tilting foot bridges are the only way to the far side of the stream, and home. ◉ There are few stops along this stretch of highway, through the river towns of Hot Springs and Marshall and on over to Mars Hill and

Nobie Brachens' sense of humor is as deft as her artistry—she refers to herself as one of "the hooker sisters".

With Each Hand Different

Burnsville. But what you will gather is a sense of place. Take your time. ⑥ Driving along this side of Spruce Pine, you'll soon find yourself in the gravitational pull of the Penland School, one of the great shapers of the American craft movement. In a certain way, Penland represents both hallowed ground and new frontier. In textiles. In glass. In ironwork. In photography as craft. In the traditional zen of throwing and glazing pottery. ⑥ The school radiates energy. And so does the work that comes out of it. In its shops and classrooms, and in studios and fine galleries that dot the surrounding region, you will be drawn toward pieces of amazing beauty, whimsy, and charm. ⑥ Up the Toe River, in and around Spruce Pine, at Little Switzerland, down in Marion, and throughout the storied town of Black Mountain, the remaining half of the Circle The Mountain loop offers hundreds of opportunities to appreciate the influence of Miss Lucy's Penland. And the influence of craftspeople who come by their craft in the most natural and cherished of ways. Handed down, one generation to the next, with each hand different.

Circle the Mountain

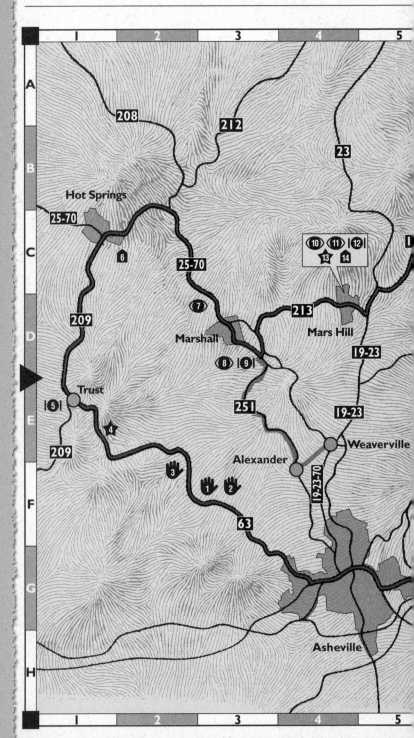

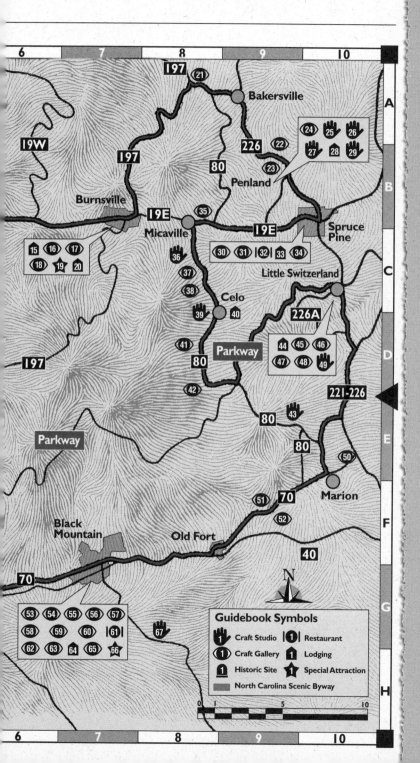

19W

197

197 (21)

Bakersville

226 (22)

(24) (25) (26)
(27) (28) (29)

80
(23)

Penland

Burnsville

19E (35)

Micaville

19E

Spruce
Pine

(15) (16) (17)
(18) (19) (20)

(30) (31) (32) (33) (34)

Little Switzerland

(36)

(37)

(38)

Celo

226A

(39) (40)

(44) (45) (46)
(47) (48) (49)

197

(41)

Parkway

80

(42)

221-226

80 (43)

Parkway

80

(50)

(51) **70**

Marion

Black
Mountain

Old Fort

(52)

40

70

(53) (54) (55) (56) (57)
(58) (59) (60) (61)
(62) (63) (64) (65) (66)

(67)

N

Guidebook Symbols

1 Craft Studio |1| Restaurant

(1) Craft Gallery   1 Lodging

1 Historic Site   1 Special Attraction

North Carolina Scenic Byway

0 1   5   10

This tour rambles through hilly, often mountainous countryside, making for a driving trail of approximately 215 miles. A three-day itinerary is strongly recommended.

Begin in Asheville, proceed out Patton Avenue (19/23 South) to Leicester Highway (NC 63). Drive through small, upcountry farms, up over Doggett Mountain and into the Spring Creek Valley. At the outset, stops are few but the beauty of the countryside makes this early-going especially memorable.

Two views at Herb of Grace.

Messages stack up at the Trust General Store bulletin board.

Earl Stressing's three-dimensional wood art.

OUT OF ASHEVILLE

1 Renaissance Glass DRIVE 8.5 MILES ON LEICESTER HWY TO ALEXANDER RD. THEN 2.4 MILES. Frank Daniels keeps designing new stained glass shapes and color combinations to satisfy collectors of the sun's rays. He can put the eyes on a spider. Mon–Fri, 9–4. (704) 683-1479

2 Cat Jarosz Pottery TURN LEFT ONTO BEAR CREEK RD. AT THE INTERSECTION ONE-HALF MILE SOUTH OF RENAISSANCE GLASS. (Go 2.9 miles to driveway marked by concrete rabbits.) One-time student of Elma Johnson at UNCA shows the influence of the master teacher. Thurs–Fri, 12–5. (704) 683-3747

3 Ralph Gates 8 WILLOW CREEK RD. TURN LEFT AT TRADING POST FROM HWY 63, six miles up and over Earley Mountain into Sandy Mush Valley. Broommaker. Mon–Fri, 10–5. (704) 683-9521

4 Herb of Grace ON NC 63, TWO MILES SHY OF TRUST. A cottage of exquisite charm surrounded by herb gardens of color and fragrance. Spring Creek chatters pleasantly nearby. Fri–Sat, 10–6; Sun, 12–6 (mid-March to mid-Dec). (704) 622-7319

5 The Spring Creek Cafe JUNCTION OF 63 AND 209, TRUST. Fresh trout and butterscotch pie in a place natural to such wonders. Mon–Sat, 11:30–8; Sun, 11:30–7. (704) 622-7412

6 Duckett House Inn and Farm. HIGHWAY 209, COMING INTO HOT SPRINGS. Victorian manor house on five acres bordering Spring Creek and within a shout of the Appalachian Trail. Six guest rooms plus tent camping. Garden fresh meals. (704) 622-7621

7 Brush Creek Mountain Arts and Crafts At press time, after it was too late to update, we learned that Brush Creek Mountain Arts and Crafts had closed. Sorry for the confusion.

The Road Goes On Forever
Side Trips, adventures, and treasure hunts

The Madison County Courthouse in Marshall is improbably sandwiched between river's edge and a high mountain spine.

8 **Jim Boylan, sculptor** Metal sculptures, largely figurines, accessible to public at the Marshall House, overlooking the town of Marshall and the French Broad River. This historic residence is open seven days a week. (704) 649 2999

0 **The Rock Cafe** MAIN ST., MARSHALL. A fine little restaurant just a stone's throw from the river. Neighbors speak highly of the roast pork with apple cider sauce. Open Mon–Fri, 11–2:30; Thur–Sat, 5–9, with local music. (704) 649-3810

Watch out for this serpent by Mike Glenn at the Madison Herb Store.

MARS HILL

10 **Madison Herb Store** AT NC 213 AND MAIN ST. IN MARS HILL. Handcrafted gifts, herb products, and the work of Nobie Brachens. Mon–Fri, 9:30–5, year-round except February. (704) 689-5974

11 **The Gallery** TWO DOORS DOWN FROM MADISON HERB STORE. Local and regional crafts displayed in an inviting storefront location. Mon–Fri, 10–5; Sat, 10–4. (704) 689-5520

12 **The Nostalgia Cafe** NEXT DOOR TO THE GALLERY ON MAIN. The name says it. Literally thousands of do-dads, knickknacks and memories hang on the walls. Mon–Fri, 9am–2pm. (704) 689-9556.

13 **The Rural Life Museum** ONE BLOCK WEST OF MAIN ON MARS HILL COLLEGE CAMPUS. Ivy-covered stone building once part of the college, now dedicated to preserving mountain farm and

A loom at rest inside the Rural Life Museum.

You'll find this folk art by Christopher and Sherry Troxell at Hayden Gallery.

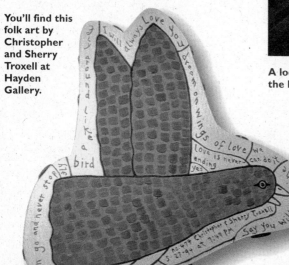

Early this century, wild indigo was the base for all blue dyes used in the mountains.

Guidebook Symbols

 Craft Studio   Restaurant

Craft Gallery   Lodging

Historic Site   Special Attraction

A "money pockets" quilt by Eliza Rollins Hensley, on display at the Rural Life Museum.

craft culture. Visually compelling recreations of hearth and home, exhibits of farm and craft implements and techniques, historic photographic murals, all supported by scholarly documentation. Mon–Fri, 2–4 during school year. Also open one hour before Southern Appalachian Repertory Theater performances. (704) 689-1424

14 **The Baird House Bed & Breakfast** 41 SOUTH MAIN ST. Known for generous breakfasts and a graceful architecture that's survived all these years since Dr. Baird's patients built the place for his family in the 1890s. Open year-round, except December. (704) 689-5722

BURNSVILLE

15 **Nu-Wray Inn** TOWN SQUARE, BURNSVILLE. Founded in 1833, this rambling three story structure with its expansive front porch fairly oozes hospitality. Famous for family-style breakfasts and dinners. The 26 rooms squeak with period furniture. Modest but tasteful craft display in lobby. Listed on National Register of Historic Places. (704) 682-2329, (800) 368-9729

16 **Hayden Gallery** ONE BLOCK OFF SQUARE ON S. MAIN ST., BURNSVILLE. A stimulating environment of contemporary work, drawing the support of local craftspeople and patronage of regional collectors. Worthy of at least ten "Ah-hah's." Open Mon–Sat, 10–5. (704) 682-7998

Sit a spell on the front porch of the Nu-Wray Inn.

17 **The Country Peddler** 3 TOWN SQUARE, BURNSVILLE. Custom-made quilts and supplies. Mon–Sat, 9–5. (704) 682-7810

18 **Something Special** 102 W. MAIN ST., BURNSVILLE. Gifts and crafts. Mon–Sat, 9–6. (704) 682-9101

19 **Needle-Me-This** 112 W. MAIN ST., BURNSVILLE. Quilting items and quilting instruction. Mon–Sat, 9:30–5. (704) 682-9462

20 **Terrell House Bed & Breakfast** TWO BLOCKS OFF TOWN SQUARE. A colonial-style inn, once a dormitory for school girls. Breakfast with crystal and china. (704) 682-4505

21 **David Boone, wood carver** NINE MILES OUT OF BURNSVILLE OFF OF NC 197 S ON PENSACOLA ROAD. A beautiful drive along a rushing stream takes you toward Mt. Mitchell and this award-winning carver's gallery. Life-size wooden bear on front porch indicates that you've arrived. Mon–Sat, 10–5 (June–Sept). (704) 682-2838

The many faces of William Bernstein.

The Road Goes On Forever
Side Trips, adventures, and treasure hunts

SCULPTURE FOUNTAIN AT MARS HILL
Designed by Douglas Ferguson to honor the quilt makers of Yancey County. Each tile square represents a classic quilt pattern. Ferguson drew from his experiences growing up in nearby Possum Trot.

BAKERSVILLE

(22) Snow Creek Pottery BETWEEN SPRUCE PINE AND BAKERSVILLE. Turn left off NC 226 at sign marked "To Slagle Road." Stay left. Deep-hued pottery practical enough for kitchen use, attractive enough to show off. Mon–Sat, 9–5; Sun, 12–5. (704) 688-3196

(23) Sedberry Clay Studio 47 MINE CREEK ROAD, SOUTH OF BAKERSVILLE OFF NC 226. A turn-of-the-century farm site offering turn-of-the-next-century craft: vibrant tiles, bowls, plates, and cups. Visually stimulating. Mon–Sat, 10–5. (704) 688-3386

PENLAND AREA

(24) Penland Gallery THE "CAMPUS" STORE FOR PENLAND, JUST AT THE CREST OF THE HILL APPROACHING THE SCHOOL. Totally out of the ordinary crafts exhibited for sale. Most are products of mentors, teachers, and artisans of Penland, recognized as one of the finest crafts schools in America. Some of this work is guaranteed to knock your socks off. Tues–Sat, 10–12 and 1–4:30; Sun, 12–4 (April–Dec). (704) 765-2359

(25) Bringle Pottery Studio GRAVEL DRIVE ACROSS FROM GALLERY. Functional and architectural pieces. The potter invites you to watch as she creates large plates and bowls in natural shades. Year-round, 10–5. (704) 765-0240

Top: Stair railing at Penland by metal sculptor Rick Smith.

Above: The Weaving Cabin at Penland.

(26) Barking Spider Pottery CAMPUS ROAD TO END OF PAVEMENT, TURN RIGHT, .75 MILES TO PAVED DRIVE ON LEFT. Contemporary residence conceals studio and gallery below. This light, airy space is a delight. Enjoy the scenery while you browse among festive ornaments and useful earth-toned pottery. Year-round, 9–5. (704) 765-2670

(27) Jane Peiser Studio CAMPUS ROAD TO END OF PAVEMENT, TURN LEFT DOWN GRAVEL ROAD TO BOTTOM. Hand built colored porcelain. Brightly colored figurines of distinction created in a garden environment. Nationally recognized. Mon–Sat, 9:30–4:30; Sun, 1–4:30. (704) 765-7123

(28) Chinquapin Inn at Penland A 1937 mountain house with stone fireplace, sun porches, and garden paths. (704) 765-0064.

(29) The Pottery, studio and gallery PENLAND ROAD. Functional pottery with "fish scale" glaze is a specialty. Daily, 9–6. (704) 765-8222

Backtrack to NC 226, following it into Spruce Pine to Locust Ave.

Barking Spider employee Andi Steel.

SPOT IT! It's somewhere on this loop. Can you find it?

Guidebook Symbols

Craft Studio		Restaurant	
Craft Gallery		Lodging	
Historic Site		Special Attraction	

Coils of color by Nancy Keller

SPRUCE PINE

(30) **Lower Street Market** 217 LOCUST AVE., SPRUCE PINE. Renovated older building divided into stalls and used as co-op for a variety of folk craft. One such stall, Promises, offers dried arrangements and painted furniture. Mon–Thurs, 10–6; Fri–Sat, 10–8. (704) 765-5683

(31) **Twisted Laurel Gallery** 333 LOCUST AVE., SPRUCE PINE. An inspired collection of glass from artists such as John Littleton, Kate Vogel, Gary Beecham. Most pieces made within a 25-mile radius of Spruce Pine. Clockmaker Luther Stroup, an owner, often drops by with a story or two. Tue–Sat, 10–5 (April–Dec); Fri–Sat, 10–5 (Jan–March). (704) 765-1562

Stunning glass art by Judi Weilbacher.

"Tractor Seat" by William Edwards.

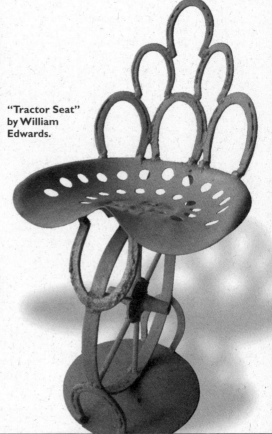

Bobby Phillips turned this wood vessel.

The Road Goes On Forever
Side Trips, adventures, and treasure hunts

SHELTON'S SILVER
Near White Rock, in the early 1800's, "Duck" Shelton was publicly whipped for making coins from a secret silver mine. Duck, whose mine has never been rediscovered, hunted squirrels with silver bullets.

32 **Cedar Crest Restaurant** 311 LOCUST ST. Homemade desserts and neighborhood news. (704) 765-6124

33 **Richmond Inn** 101 PINE AVE. A wood-frame and stone building from 1939 offering a full southern breakfast. (704) 765-6993

34 **Woody's Chair Shop** INTERSECTION OF 226 AND DALE RD., JUST SOUTH OF SPRUCE PINE. Third generation chair maker operating in the same location as his grandfather. First generation quality. Chairs are primary focus, but you will also find walking sticks, boxes and kitchen utensils. In the early 1960s the family sent small rocking chairs to the Kennedy children. Mon–Fri, 8–5; Sat, 9–4 (May–Dec); Sat only (Jan–April). (704) 765-9277

A "chorus" of bell ornaments at Barking Spider.

TOE RIVER/CELO AREA

35 **Micaville Store and Gallery** JUNCTION OF US 19 E AND NC 80. A craft co-op and an antique dealer share a charming space inside the old Micaville General Store. The opportunity to look for handcrafted older items and contemporary crafts is both the challenge and the fun of this stop. Mon–Sat, 9–5; Sun, 1–5 (May–Oct); Fri–Sat, 10–5, (Dec). (704) 675-9143

36 **Ian and Jo Lydia Craven Pottery** 1692 NC 80, TWO MILES SOUTH FROM MICAVILLE. Striking hand built porcelains impressed with heirloom lace. Galleries from Madrid to Munich have exhibited the work of this husband and wife team. Mon–Sat, 10–5, April–Dec. (704) 675-9058 or (800) 764-2402

37 **The Candlelight** 3155 NC 80, FOUR MILES SOUTH OF MICAVILLE. Especially nice stained glass, from sun-catchers to custom windows. Daily, 9–5 (June–Oct). (704) 675-4189

38 **Craft Pride Gallery** 3961 NC 80. Represents several local crafters. A select collection of glass, wearable art, pottery, wood and candles. Working pottery studio on site. Mon–Sat, 10–5. (704) 675-5470

Richard Kennedy's evocative sandstone casting.

39 **McWhirter Pottery** 4088 NC 80, SIX MILES SOUTH OF MICAVILLE. A family-operated gallery and studio, featuring simple, decorative, cherished designs. Mon–Sat, 10–5. (704) 675-4559

40 **Celo Inn** ABOUT SEVEN MILES SOUTH OF MICAVILLE. Within walking distance of several studios. A charming timber-frame bed & breakfast in harmony with its surroundings. Reservations required. (704) 675-5132

Guidebook Symbols

 Craft Studio   Restaurant

Craft Gallery   Lodging

Historic Site   Special Attraction

**"Divine Intervention"
by Dan Howachyn.**

(41) Toe River Crafts 7.5 MILES SOUTH OF MICAVILLE ON NC 80. Crafts of the Toe River community. From fresh and whimsical to the traditional. A co-operative venture managed by members, in a very personal manner. Tues–Sat, 10–5; Sun 12–5 (June–Aug, and Oct); Sat–Sun, 12–5 (May and Sept).

(42) Sharpless Pottery FROM NC 80, TURN ONTO SEVEN MILE RIDGE ROAD, THEN LEFT ON GRAVEL ROUTE 1225 FOR ONE MILE. Functional, everyday pottery of good quality. Mugs in whites, blues, and browns. Daily, 10–5 with gallery. (704) 765-7809

(43) Buck Creek Bowls ON NC 80, FOUR MILES SOUTH OF INTERSECTION WITH PARKWAY. Return to Parkway to continue trail. Wood vessels, deftly made of trees native to Western North Carolina. Demonstrations and hands-on instruction. Daily, 9–5 (June 1–Sept 10). (704) 724-9048

LITTLE SWITZERLAND

(44) Switzerland Inn AT MILEPOST 334 ON THE PARKWAY. A sprawling, fanciful hotel plucked from the Alps with wonderful meals and a view to match. On a clear day, you can practically see Europe. Closed in winter only. (800) 654-4026

(45) The Trillium Gallery AT THE BLUE RIDGE PARKWAY AND 226 A ON THE GROUNDS OF THE INN. A high altitude collection of exquisite regional work. Distinctive pottery and glass pieces, along with handmade jewelry. Daily, 10–5 (May–Oct). (704) 765-0024

(46) Hearthside Handmades AT SWITZERLAND INN. Well worth visiting for the wovens, dolls, and carvings. Mon–Sat, 9–5 (May–Oct). (704) 765-7982

(47) The Busy B's ANOTHER SHOP AT THE INN. Quilts and hem-stitched linens. Daily, 10–5 (May–Oct). (704) 765-5411

(48) Pine Crossing ON NC 226, LESS THAN A HALF MILE NORTH OF THE PARKWAY. Local pottery and woodcrafts. Tues–Sat, 10–5 (April–Nov). (704) 765-8400

(49) Bea Hensley and Son Hand Forge ON NC 226 AT THE PARKWAY. 15th and 16th century black-smithing by masters. Bea also knows every good trout stream in the mountains. Mon–Fri, 9–5.

TOWARD OLD FORT

(50) Blue Ridge Country Crafts DOWN 226 FROM LITTLE SWITZERLAND TO 221 AT WOODLAWN.

The Road Goes On Forever

Side Trips, adventures, and treasure hunts

LITTLE BROWN JUG
In the mountain economy, corn brought a higher price in liquid form than it did in the husk. And the handiest container was the little brown jug. Potters flourished during Prohibition crafting distinctive jugware for the trade.

Family-produced folk craft. Daily, 10–6. (704) 756-4221

⑤1 **Max Woody's Chair Shop** US 70 AT PLEASANT GARDENS, BETWEEN MARION AND OLD FORT. Behind those dusty windows are rows of handcrafted rocking chairs of the finest quality. Hours irregular, but with good intentions. (704) 724-4158

⑤2 **Garrou Pottery** US 70 AT PLEASANT GARDENS, straight across from Woody's Chair. Value-priced, globally useful pottery in myriad shapes. Ovenproof, dishwasher and microwave safe. Mon–Sat, 10–5:30. (704) 724-4083

INTO BLACK MOUNTAIN

⑤3 **Black Mountain Iron Works** 120 BROADWAY. Forged iron pieces for home and garden, including "yard whimsies" of grand charm. Practical pieces for the hearth. Mon–Sat, 10–5; Sun, 1–5. (704) 669-1001

⑤4 **The Phoenix** 104 W. STATE ST. A working studio and gallery where Julie Bauer's fused glass pieces will surely get your attention. Also hand-painted bright silks. Mon–Fri, 10–5; Sat, 10–6; Sun, 1–5. (704) 669-4045

⑤5 **Giftcrafts** 114 W. STATE ST. Crafts, collectibles, and antiques. Mon–Sat, 10–5. (704) 669-8217

"Dance to Joy" by William Bernstein.

Guidebook Symbols

🤚1 Craft Studio |◉| Restaurant
◉1 Craft Gallery   🏠1 Lodging
🏛1 Historic Site   ⭐1 Special Attraction

Special delivery: Iron and copper mailbox by Dan Howachyn, Black Mt. Iron Works.

(56) Black Bear Craft Shoppe 116 WEST STATE ST. Traditional crafts of the Swannanoa Valley. Mon–Sat, 10–5. (704) 669-0069

(57) Old Depot Association SUTTON AVE. Non-profit arts and crafts gallery with over 75 craftspeople represented. Baskets, pottery, weaving, train whistles. Mon–Sat, 10–5 (April–Dec). (704) 669-6583

(58) Cherry Street Gallery 132 CHERRY ST. A range of crafts—glass, pottery, jewelry, iron, wood—from within and without the mountain region. Mon–Sat, 10–5; Sun, 1–5. (704) 669-0450

(59) Seven Sisters 117 CHERRY ST. A treasure house. Wonderful splashes of color—whether shawls, kaleidoscopes, wood carvings, porcelains, wall hangings, place settings, or imaginings. In all, over 200 artisans presented. Mon–Sat, 10–5; Sun, 1–5. (704) 669-5107

(60) Thyme And Again 105 CHERRY ST. Crafts and collectibles. Mon–Sat, 11–5. (704) 669-5981

(61) Church Street Crossing 102 CHURCH ST. Espresso, teas, and biscotti in the company of nice folks and the work of local artists. Mon–Sat, 8:30–9; Sun, 10–6. (704) 669-1626

(62) Song Of The Wood 203 W. STATE ST. Hammered dulcimers and psalters started from scratch and ending in song. Plenty of help and advice on the premises of a beautifully renovated building. Mon–Sat, 10–5. (704) 669-7675

(63) Black Mountain Gallery 207 W. STATE ST. Handmade bowls, often in exotic shapes and rare woods, crafted by father and son. Demonstrations on site. Seven days, 10–5. (704) 669-2450

(64) Monte Vista Hotel 400 BLOCK, W. STATE ST. Established 1919 and run pretty much the same way ever since. Hospitality reigns, along with legendary Sunday lunches. White linens, fresh flowers, and oftentimes piano music. The chess pie wins. Seven days. (704) 669-2119

"The Swing" by sculptor Jim Boylan.

The Road Goes On Forever

Side Trips, adventures, and treasure hunts

THE ONE FINGER WAVE
Two hands on the wheel are recommended for most mountain driving. But local custom dictates that you wave to every one you pass. The solution? The One Finger Wave. Neighborly. And easy to master.

(65) **Vern & Idy's** 414 W. STATE ST. Lots of stuff, including pottery, fiber arts, glass, carved pieces, and dolls in a friendly, refreshing environment. Lori Kemp will point you in the right direction. Tues–Sat, 12–5. (704) 669-2370

(66) **Red Rocker Country Inn** 136 DOUGHERTY ST. Renowned for breakfast. Vast platters of food with heavenly origins. Over such a breakfast, strangers can wind up lifelong friends. (704) 669-5991

OUT OF BLACK MOUNTAIN

(67) **Eula Mae Lavender** ABOUT NINE MILES OUT RT. 9 (A SCENIC BYWAY), TOWARD BAT CAVE. A cottage by a stream where Eula Mae displays quilts she and her friends have made along with afghans, stoles, and throws. Warm pieces and good company. Mon–Fri, 10–5. (704) 669-2188

TO ASHEVILLE

(68) **Folk Art Center** AT PARKWAY MILEPOST 382 NEAR US 70 IN OTEEN. Home of historic Allanstand Craft Shop, one of the early retail co-ops in the Appalachian region. Hundreds of artful pieces in virtually all media produced by members of the Southern Highland Craft Guild. A moveable feast of special exhibits in the gallery by individual artisans. The building also houses the Guild's craft library and a theater for seasonal productions. Demonstrations outside and inside, spring through fall color. Mon–Sat, 9:30–5:30. Also open Sun, 12–5 (Oct–Dec). (704) 298-7928

"Corinthian" by Tom McGlauchlin.

French Broad Overview

Take an interesting side trip by heading south out of Marshall on Route 251 to Alexander. This ten mile stretch parallels the French Broad, a river in a hurry and going the wrong way. It flows north. Cyclists, paddlers, and trains also wind through this verdant river valley on a predictable basis.

Step 1   *Step 2*

Guidebook Symbols

Craft Studio		Restaurant	
Craft Gallery		Lodging	
Historic Site		Special Attraction	

Penland School

Hallowed Ground and New Frontier

Penland fulfills three criteria for being a wonderful place to learn. First, it is isolated, cloistered from the distractions of the everyday world. Secondly, personal needs, like food and lodging, are provided for. And, finally, it is a place that encourages the deepest and most intimate expressions of the heart.

This may not be the way Miss Lucy Morgan would have described the school she founded in 1929. But there is no doubt she would approve of what has transpired since she first brought together mountain women to rekindle the art of hand weaving in a modest cabin, a gathering place constructed by mountain neighbors with logs signed and donated as individual gifts.

The Penland of today is a place where you can immerse yourself so deeply in craft that time becomes practically immaterial. Studio doors stay open day and night. Professionals and beginners, teenagers and octagenerians, sit side by side in classes. Secrets are freely shared. And the only competition you'll encounter is over the last dish of cobbler at dinner.

Top: Basketmaking at Penland in the late 1920s. Bottom: Working on the Craft House — a large log structure still in use today built by neighbors with donated logs.

Miss Lucy Morgan and Howard C. Ford with the cabin that was taken to the 1932 Worlds Fair in Chicago.

The credit for this celebratory, open, affirming atmosphere circles back to Bill Brown, who was Miss Lucy's hand-picked choice for director when she retired in 1962. Brown expanded the curriculum and broadened its scope, turning the school into an international destination. Among students from Bolivia, Japan, and Germany, the most likely common language is craft.

Bill Brown also made Penland a destination for instructors. He used a very simple formula – teach what you like, bring your families, and take advantage of instruction for yourself, inside or outside your own discipline.

A potter loading a kiln in the 30s.

These days, offerings span a diverse range of classes, from neon to functional teapots. There are eight different core areas: textiles, ceramics, glass, metals, wood, photography, printmaking, and books, with many classes making connections between media. In glass, for example, the work of Penland graduates appears in the galleries of London, Zurich, Tokyo, and Milan. But in all these media, the name Penland gives off its own special aura—the kinship of a place and a time where the imaginings of the heart transform into something you can touch.

farm to Market

The craft of this loop trail is a craft of southern towns, courthouse squares, and the circular seasons of the farm. ❀ You won't find heavy concentrations of craftspeople—potters or glassmakers, for example—but you will find a merging and mingling of many works of hand across a rumpled landscape of orchards and cotton fields. ❀ It's a handwork of straw wreaths and paper angels, bird houses and apple butter. Kudzu jelly and fig preserves. Apples, pumpkins, and walnuts. And things you take home, but never buy. Like the pitch of a Victorian farmhouse. Or a mainstreet overhung with magnolias. Orchards that crowd against the back of country stores. Farmers' markets, and courthouses with silvery domes. ❀ Near Rutherfordton, you'll enter into a belt of warmer air—a zone where warm air tends to pool up, tempering the seasons, making them more reminiscent of the Deep South than the high mountains (less than two hours north). This

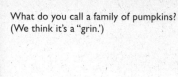

What do you call a family of pumpkins?
(We think it's a "grin.")

A Slow Dance up Main

delightful phenomenon makes it possible to grow cotton and peaches and to encounter courthouse lawns full of blooms when you wouldn't expect to see them. ❦ Valdese is a short hop from Morganton, on a spur from the loop, but this unusual town is more than worth the trip. There is enough history between its bocci courts and stone schoolhouse to fill an entire travel journal. ❦ Small towns are the way of this loop tour. And they're all distinctly their own. In Forest City, for example, you will drive down a main avenue divided by trees in a kind of linear park. Small shops, eateries and mercantiles open their doors to the street along both sides, reminiscent of, well, pick a decade. ❦ Between towns, the highway skims along by farms and homesteads and through wide places and crossroads that might attract a store or two or, in season, a fruitstand ripe with color. We advise you adjust to the proper rhythm: you'll need to slow dance your way through this one.

farm to Market

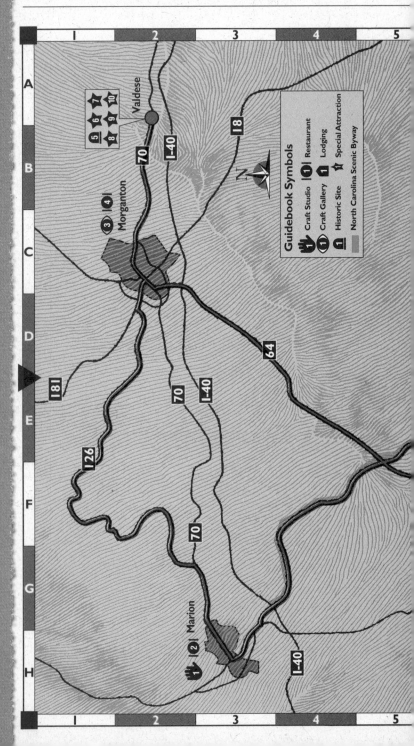

Valdese

5 6 7 10
8 9

70 I-40

18

Morganton

3 4

Guidebook Symbols

Craft Studio   Restaurant
Craft Gallery   Lodging
Historic Site   Special Attraction
North Carolina Scenic Byway

N

64

181

126 70 I-40

70

Marion

1 2

I-40

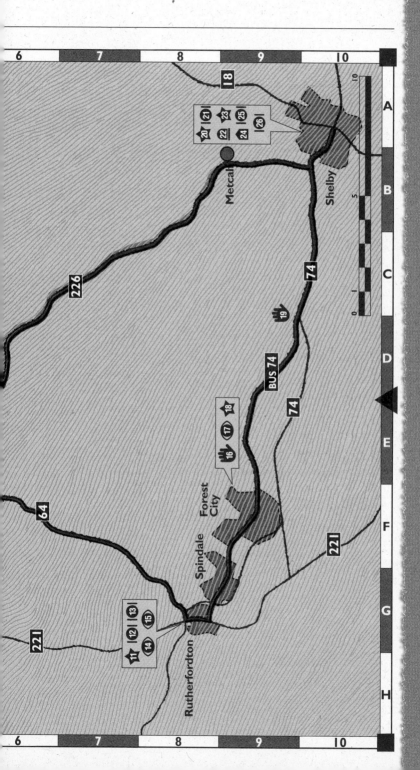

6 7 8 9 10

18

A

20 21 23 25
22 24 26

Metcalf

Shelby

B

226

74

C

19

D

BUS 74

74

18
16 17

E

Spindale
Forest
City

F

64

221

G

221

12 13
11 14 15

Rutherfordton

H

6 7 8 9 10

Enter the Farm To Market loop by proceeding down US 221 from the Parkway, arriving in Marion on its northwest side. Leaving Marion on "Farm to Market" and returning to Marion, you'll cover about 150 miles and, at a leisurely pace, about two days.

Somewhere off the beaten path

IN MARION

1 **Catawba River Pottery** HWY 70 JUST WEST OF MARION AT ROBY CONLEY ROAD IN A STONE HOUSE. Marjorie Pittman, pottery maker and noted pottery historian, creates pieces that celebrate rural life. Mon–Sat, 10–5 (May–December). (704) 724-4995

2 **Josephine's Cafe** 206 HILLCREST DR. A beautifully restored, turn-of-the-century mansion with expansive porches and well-presented lunches that include freshly-baked breads and desserts. Listed on the National Register. Monday–Friday, 11–3. (704) 659-3374

Leaving Marion, drive to Nebo (and the lake of the same name) along Hwy 70, then swing off onto Route 126 skirting along Lake James and down into Morganton.

IN MORGANTON

3 **South Mountain Crafts** 409 ENOLA ROAD. A collection of cottages where handicapped residents of Western Carolina Center make frontier furniture and craft pieces. The only NC teaching facility of its kind where handcrafted objects are clearly the focus. Your purchase will help insure the program's future. Mon–Fri, 8:30–4. (704) 433-2836

4 **Judge's Riverside** AT GREENLEE FORD ON THE CATAWBA RIVER. A rambling smokehouse barbecue place where you can sit inside or out-of-doors under spreading walnut trees on a deck above the river. In either case, you can basically pig out. Every day, lunch and dinner. (704) 433-5798

VALDESE

Unmistakably worth a few hours departure from the trail—especially since you will be driving from Morganton into Northern Italy.

5 **Waldensian Church** MAIN ST. Originally built of fieldstone and true grit. Each year here, the Waldensians celebrate the end of three centuries of persecution with a special service honoring the 1848 Edict of Emancipation issued by King Alberto of Italy. Visitors welcome. Mon–Fri, 9–5. (704) 874-2531

> *We abuse land because we regard it as a commodity belonging to us. When we see land as a community to which we belong, we may begin to use it with love and respect.*
>
> Aldo Leopold

The Road Goes On Forever
Side Trips, adventures, and treasure hunts

ALL THAT'S WALDENSIAN.
In 1893, a group of 29 Northern Italians arrived in Western North Carolina in search of a home in America. The town of Valdese, with its streets named for early families—Praly, Rodoret, Colombo, Ribet—is a testament to their enterprise and faith.

6 **Waldensian Museum** JUST DOWN THE HILL FROM THE CHURCH. A museum that's really a journey of families, each generation a part of the historical mosaic of Valdese. This inviting place features memorabilia from both the Italian and American experience: Waldensian dress and handmade linens, references to the trip over—from steamships to carried traditions—and the story of this community since 1893 to include bakery, hosiery mill, and winery. Sundays, 3 to 5pm (April–Oct), or ask at the church office any day of the week and a docent will open the door for your party.

Inside the Waldensian Museum

7 **Valdese Public Library** JUST OFF MAIN ST. Inside, large stained glass works depict the traditional dress of the Waldensians and the fruits of their New World labor.

8 **Old Rock School** MAIN ST. Classic turn-of-the-century rock schoolhouse built of fieldstone cleared from farm land. The building boasts a renovated auditorium, art exhibits, and a surprisingly large and detailed miniature train system that depicts the trip to Asheville and west. Holds Community Affairs Office. (704) 879-2129

9 **Villar Vintners of Valdese** ON VILLAR LANE, JUST OFF NORTH LAUREL ST. The only spot in North Carolina where the production of wine was legal during prohibition. Tour and tasting hours: Thurs, Fri, Sat, 10–6; Sun, 1–6. (704) 879-3202

10 **Old Colony Players Amphitheater** CHURCH ST. Site of "From This Day Forward," historical Waldensian Drama. First and second weekends in August. For ticket information, (704) 874-0176.

After returning to Morganton via Hwy 70, turn south on US Route 64, driving roughly 30 miles to Rutherfordton through rolling country, meandering streams, and barn-dotted farmland.

IN RUTHERFORDTON

11 **Main street murals** The work of Clive Haynes, an artist brought up in England who continues to turn Rutherfordton into something else. You can't miss these wall-size scenes if you stroll the downtown—especially if you mistakenly walk into one, in which case you will be abruptly halted. Main Street Rutherfordton is listed in the National Register of Historic Places.

12 **Anything Goes** 215 N. MAIN ST. Notable for its lunchtime hospitality and Clive Hayne's New Orleans panorama up the stairs to the rear of the place. (704) 286-2555

Clive Haynes and one of his streetscapes

Guidebook Symbols

Craft Studio	Restaurant
Craft Gallery	Lodging
Historic Site	Special Attraction

DEEP SOUTH.
Green River Plantation. From US 221 south of Rutherfordton, turn right on Coxe Road and drive 2.7 miles. Built in 1804, with bricks and hand-carved mantles hauled up from Charleston. Hoof prints of Union Army horses imprint the heart-pine floors. National Register. Mon, 10-5. Adults $10. (704) 287-0983

If you know what this is, call the Rutherford County Farm Museum. They're just as curious as we are.

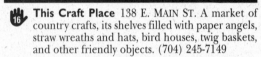

|13| **57 Alpha Cafe** AT THE RUTHERFORDTON AIRPORT. A pilot's favorite and worth the drive even if you're grounded. Known in these parts for homemade chili, banana pudding, limonade (made of limes and lemons), and country ham. Lunch only, Tues–Sat, 10–3. (704) 286-1677

(14) **Real Toys USA** 12B MORGANTON RD. A shop where wooden dump trucks, cranes, wreckers, and other child-powered vehicles, usually a couple of feet in length, are made to last several childhoods. Drop by weekdays to see the fleet. (704) 286-1755

(15) **Conniedon Art & Craft** US 221 NORTH OF RUTHERFORDTON. Something of the usual, represented by traditional quilts, along with something of the unusual, represented by paintings on saw blades. Tues–Sat, 10 to 4:30. (704) 287-9634

Leave Rutherfordton on US 74 B for a short drive to Forest City, through Ellenboro, then onto Shelby.

FOREST CITY

16 **This Craft Place** 138 E. MAIN ST. A market of country crafts, its shelves filled with paper angels, straw wreaths and hats, bird houses, twig baskets, and other friendly objects. (704) 245-7149

(17) **Odds N Ends Crafts** 238 E. MAIN ST. Handmade pleasantries, including wreaths and rugs from the neighborhood. Mon–Sat, 10–3. (704) 245-6162

18 **Rutherford County Farm Museum** 240 DEPOT ST. Left-handed plows and livermush paddles. Hair straighteners and wooden refrigerators. Rope beds, homemade radios and molasses skimmers. If you've ever heard a story about the farm, this place will decorate it with implements of a lost time. Wed–Sat, 10 to 4. $2 for adults. (704) 248-1248

On the way to Shelby, in Mooresboro

19 **Douglas Carlisle, cabinetmaker** 111 LAHRMER LANE. Furniture restorations and new pieces with an emphasis on 18th century design and joinery. Mon–Fri, 8:30am to 5:30pm. (704) 434-5204

IN SHELBY

20 **Shelby Farmer's Market** 299 W. WARREN ST. Handpicked fruits and vegetables in season and home-baked breads, pies, and cakes, all sheltered in a colonial revival warehouse next to the railroad tracks. Tues–Sat, 8–6. (704) 484-6829

|21| **McCoy's Cafe** INSIDE THE FARMER'S MARKET, 211 W. WARREN ST. Fried livermush tops the menu

The Road Goes On Forever
Side Trips, adventures, and treasure hunts

some days along with black-eyed peas and fried sauerkraut. Tues–Fri, breakfast 7:30–10, lunch 11:30–2. Sat, breakfast 8–12. (704) 482-8444

22 Cleveland County Historical Museum IN THE FORMER COUNTY COURTHOUSE BUILDING AT MARION AND LAFAYETTE STREETS. Classical revival courthouse with a lawn of arching trees and, most certainly, memories. Listed on the National Register with exhibits that position Shelby in world history. Tues–Fri, 9–4. (704) 482-8186

23 The Cleveland County Arts Council ON WASHINGTON ST. ACROSS FROM THE MUSEUM. Occupies a former post office where visual arts, sculpture and craft shows feature local artists. The colonial revival building, a former post office, dates from 1916. Mon–Fri, 10–4. (704) 484-2787

24 The Inn at Webbley 403 SOUTH WASHINGTON. A historical bed and breakfast of note. Constructed in 1852 with wood art and nails made at the site. Italian market umbrellas and European antiques. A continental menu with reservations requested a day in advance. National Register. (704) 481-1403

25 Shelby Cafe 220 SOUTH LAFAYETTE ST. A 1950's two-room restaurant, with black and white tiled floors and soda fountain booths. Patrons may still talk about the weather, the cotton belt and the Iron Curtain. The photos of Shelby people are current, if it were 40 years ago. Year-round, Mon–Fri, 5am–8pm; Sat, 5am–3pm. (704) 487-8461

26 Dedmon's Livestock Restaurant 718 WALLACE GROVE DR. Livermush biscuits, fried-apple pies, fried-bologna sandwiches, and side orders of popcorn. On Tuesday you can watch livestock sales from noon til sold out. Fri–Sat, 5pm–9pm; Sun, 11am–2pm; Mon–Tues, 7am–2pm. (704) 487-8116

Leave Shelby, via 226, and return to Marion along this designated scenic highway.

HORSES OF DIFFERENT COLORS

The City of Shelby continues to restore a 1919 Herschell-Spillman Carousel that operated in City Park for three decades. See one of its horses, fully restored, at the Historical Museum.

South Mountain Scenery

Upper Piedmont farmlands of apples and corn characterize this gentle journey toward the mountains, from Shelby to Marion. To the right, around Polkville, you'll begin to glimpse the "Oakanoahs," the Cherokee's word for what we now call the South Mountains. Just into Rutherford County, Cherry Mountain emerges to the west, and later, the more abrupt face of the Appalachians appears, as if the road were destined to collide with these ancient peaks. And it does.

Forest City, with its wide boulevard and magnolias, has been named one of America's best-planned towns. In Civil War times, volunteers mustered on Main to join "Harb" Lee's company of red shirts as the band played Dixie.

Guidebook Symbols
Craft Studio   Restaurant
Craft Gallery   Lodging
Historic Site   Special Attraction

Southern Highland Craft Guild

Born on a Mountaintop

On a snowy winter's day in 1928, 11 members of the Conference of the Southern Mountain Workers gathered in the Weaver's Cabin atop Conley's Ridge at Penland School. Hosted by Miss Lucy Morgan, the group included President William J. Hutchins of Berea College, Dr. Mary Martin Sloop of the Crossnore School, Mrs. John C. Campbell from the folk school in Brasstown and "Miss Fuller," representing Francis Goodrich and the Allanstand Cottage Industries in Asheville.

When they departed two days later, they had made a guild dedicated to the conservation and development of crafts. Of course, the ground work was laid many years earlier by these same trailblazers who, through their impassioned community work, sparked a crafts revival in the mountains of Southern Appalachia.

The Guild got an early, and significant, boost thanks to the contribution by Francis Goodrich of

PHOTO COURTESY OF UNC CHAPEL HILL.

PHOTO COURTESY OF SOUTHERN HIGHLAND CRAFT GUILD

Top: Allanstand, NC c. 1910, where Allanstand Cottage Industries began with the work of Frances Goodrich. Bottom: The "Weaving Cabin" showed the first exhibition by the "Allanstand Cottage Industries Guild" in 1899.

the Allanstand Shop. She had started Allanstand in a Madison County cabin some 40 years earlier to breathe life into the craft of the mountains. By the time she made her gift, Allanstand represented the industry of many craftspeople, some of whom became Guild members.

Today, there are over 700 Guild members representing an astonishing spectrum of textures and techniques. You can get a glimpse of this eclectic outpouring at the Guild's own fairs held at the Asheville Civic Center in July and October or practically any day of the year at the Guild's Folk Art Center on the Blue Ridge Parkway.

Frances Goodrich in 1943 with the "Double Bowknot" coverlet that inspired the handycraft revival work.

PHOTO COURTESY OF SOUTHERN HIGHLAND CRAFT GUILD

The Allanstand Cottage Industries Salesroom at 55 Haywood Street in Asheville in the 1920s.

"Dream Basket" by Aunt Cord Richey, c. 1920.

PHOTO COURTESY OF SOUTHERN HIGHLAND CRAFT GUILD

Mountain Cities

Y ou should know there is something in the air here. How else would you explain such strange and wonderful behavior? *A railroad baron's grandson envisions a mountain villa and finds himself, a half-dozen years later, inviting New York friends down for a gathering at his 255-room French chateau. In the adjoining village, called "Biltmore," an industry of handcrafted items flares to life under the care and nurturance of the lady of the chateau. A successful tonic salesman builds a world class resort hotel out of boulders on the side of a mountain. And fills its rooms with custom-made "Arts and Crafts" furniture. A Spanish architect, using Moorish building techniques, constructs a Catholic church on a knoll. The church's self-supporting elliptical dome—the largest in America—consists solely of tile and concrete. A doctor from St. Louis creates a destination around a rock chimney where an elevator whooshes guests to the top for a panoramic view of the mountains. Two spirited women from the midwest sail to England at the turn of the century to study carving and needlework. They then come to the mountains of North Carolina and instruct*

Leftovers for the cat at Steebo's in Asheville.

An Irrepressible Spirit

children at Tryon's "Toy House," a copy of Anne Hathaway's home in Stratford-On-Avon.  *An architect commissioned to design Asheville's city building brings forth the red and green tones of the mountains in a cake-like, art deco masterpiece.*

You are about to follow in the footsteps of some truly audacious people who have shaped the implausible landscape of this Mountain Cities Loop. Edith and George Vanderbilt, E.W. Grove, Rafael Guastavino, Dr. Lucius Morse, Eleanor Vance and Charlotte Yale, and Douglas Ellington, among many others. The spirit of these visionary individuals, so brilliantly evident in the architecture of this loop trail, gives rise to the whole of the creative environment here. For what you will find in Asheville and Hendersonville, in Saluda, Tryon, and Columbus, and in Lake Lure, is that same urbane, beguiling attitude that makes these landmarks so stunning. It's a kind of artistic license, handed down by irrepressible people— handed down into the very hands of the artists you are about to meet, in the studios, shops and galleries along the way, where the passions of invention are a matter of physical record.

Mountain Cities

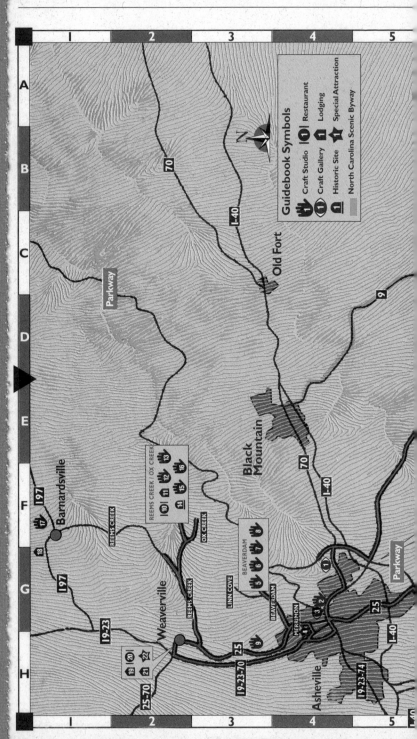

Guidebook Symbols

🖐 Craft Studio   🍽 Restaurant
① Craft Gallery   🏠 Lodging
🏛 Historic Site   ⭐ Special Attraction
▬▬ North Carolina Scenic Byway

N

Old Fort

Black Mountain

Barnardsville

Parkway

Weaverville

Asheville

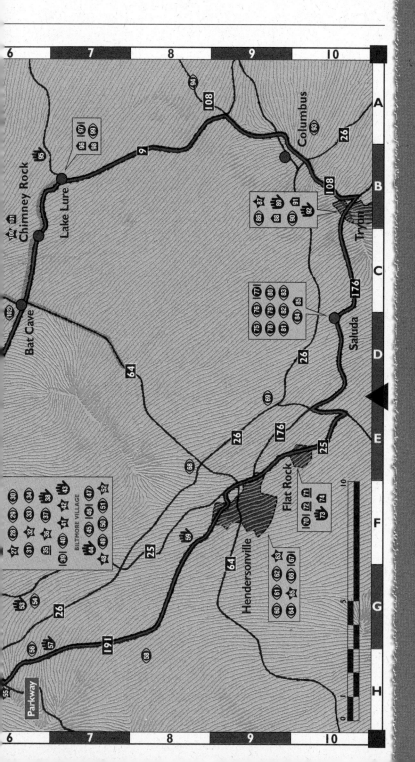

The trail begins in Asheville, heads out into northern Buncombe County, back into the city, then to Hendersonville, Saluda, Tryon, Columbus, and Lake Lure before reconnecting with your starting point. Sample only as much as you feel like tasting. With over 100 listings across 170 miles, this is the largest of the seven loop trails in this guidebook so you'll need to fashion your journey according to the time you have.

You could easily plan for an outing of several days or, taking the longer view, go ahead and move here.

EAST ASHEVILLE

1 **Folk Art Center** BLUE RIDGE PARKWAY. A good place to begin on the way to anywhere. Mon–Sat, 9:30–5:30. (See description at end of Circle the Mountain trail).

2 **Stuart Nye Hand Wrought Jewelry** 940 TUNNEL RD. Traditional silver dogwood rings and pins crafted the way Nye designed them two generations ago. View of studio. No retail sales at this location. Mon–Fri, 8–11:30 and 12:30–4. (704) 298-7988

3 **Guild Crafts** 930 TUNNEL RD. Representative offering of Southern Highland Craft Guild and Allanstand. Mon–Sat, 9:30–5:30; Sun, 12–5. (704) 298-7903

HEADING NORTH

Proceed west on Tunnel Rd. to its junction with I-240. Follow I-240 westward until it joins with 19/23, headed north. From 19/23, take the first exit, marked UNC-Asheville, driving towards the college on Broadway to a lefthand turn at Weaver Blvd.

4 **UNCA Botanical Gardens** AT BROADWAY AND WEAVER BLVD. An open, 10-acre wild flower garden site in the shape of a lazy "U," criss-crossed by footpaths and bridges and a core of volunteers who keep this place totally charming. Free and open all year for strolling. (704) 252-5190

Scenes from Bob Wager's place.

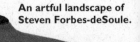

An artful landscape of Steven Forbes-deSoule.

The Road Goes On Forever

Side Trips, adventures, and treasure hunts

When Bill Nye, man of letters and humor, moved near Asheville in the 1890's, he continued to send pieces to the New York World. He wrote about the climate, his community of 37 inhabitants and eight horses...and that Wagner's music "continues to be better than it sounds."

*From Weaver Blvd, hang a left onto Merrimon Ave., driving north.
About one mile out Merrimon, turn right onto Beaverdam Rd.*

BEAVERDAM

Drive one mile to Spooks Branch Rd. Turn right.

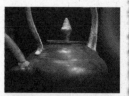

5 **Bob Wager** 82 SPOOKS BRANCH RD. Puckish master potter has a thing for pyramids and experimental glazes. Both are in abundance here, along with oil lamps and irresistible clay miniatures. He claims his unique lifetime warranty (it expires with potter) keeps people rooting for him. Check out the "Kiln Accident Corner." Mon–Sat, 10–5. (704) 253-5515

Return to Beaverdam Rd and turn right; then turn right onto Rice Branch Rd.

6 **Don Davis** 67 RICE BRANCH RD. Using a combination of throwing and coil technique, Davis fashions vases large enough to hide in. His work graces the entrance to St. John in the Wilderness Episcopal Church in Flat Rock, and the movie, "Last of the Mohicans." Evocative work rooted in prior civilizations. Fri–Sat, 10–5. (704) 251-1425

A glimpse into the world of Don Davis.

7 **George Handy** 2 WEBB COVE RD, AT THE FORK OF WEBB AND LYNN COVE. "Sketch pad" is what potter George Handy calls the swirls, dots, dashes and squiggly lines that doodle across one of his festive porcelain collections. He also specializes in cheery wall mosaics and counter tiles. Mon–Fri, 10–5. (704) 254-4691

8 **His Glassworks, Inc.** 91 WEBB COVE RD. Work as imposing as its creator, Robert Stephan. Glass globes and orbs built up, layer upon layer through the process of offhand glass blowing. Even after Robert or his wife Margaret explain the process, you'll marvel at how he does it. Mon–Fri, 11–3. (704) 254-2559

The studio of George Handy and a work in progress.

From Beaverdam Road intersection with Merrimon (Weaverville Hwy), drive 3.8 miles north to Larson's.

9 **Larson Porcelain and Design Studios** 440 WEAVERVILLE HWY. Rare art deco style building is appropriate showcase for the porcelain "Lusterware" created by Tyrone and Julie Larson. Pastels abound, along with lots of architectural pieces. Wed–Sun, 10–5. (704) 645-4777

Drive 1.2 miles north to turn-off at Reems Creek Rd.

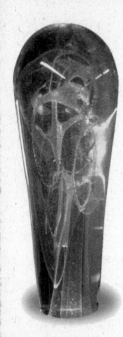

A luminous work by Robert Stephan.

REEMS CREEK

|10| **Weaverville Milling Company** REEMS CREEK RD. TURN RIGHT JUST PAST THE REEMS CREEK BRIDGE SIGN. Landmark grain mill operated 1912–1965, now a restaurant. Specials include roast pork tenderloin with apple nut dressing. Fresh rainbow trout is a standard. Seating bunches cozily around elevators and chutes of the old mill. Open six days, starting at 5pm. Closed Wednesday. (704) 645-4700

11 **Ox-Ford Farm Bed & Breakfast Inn** 75 OX CREEK RD. TAKE REEMS CREEK TO OX CREEK. TURN RIGHT. ONE HALF MILE ON RIGHT. This place embodies country life. The stone and frame farmhouse dates from the 1880s; the views from atop the surrounding meadows are eternal. Working farm is home to pedigree sheep, beef cattle, peacocks, ducks, chickens, and two adopted wild turkeys. Closed Jan–March (704) 658-2500

12 **Steven Forbes-deSoule** CONTINUE ON OX CREEK RD. TURN LEFT ON BALLARD BRANCH RD. Turn left at David Biddle Trail and follow white arrows up to #143. The earth from a satellite must look like Forbes-deSoule's globes, which are raku-fired with acrylics. Heavenly. Thurs–Fri, 12–4. (704) 645-9065

13 **Nancy Fargo Pottery** 39 BALLARD BRANCH RD. SECOND DRIVEWAY ON RIGHT PAST DAVID BIDDLE TRAIL. Rapturously elegant pottery by a recent graduate of Haywood Community College. Nancy's distinctive earth-centered work is topped off with handles of seasoned and polished laurel. New studio features a track-fed kiln that can take big sculptures and urns. Thurs–Fri, 12–4. (704) 645-2762

14 **Vance Birthplace** FIVE MILES DOWN REEMS CREEK RD. (SR 1103) FROM WEAVERVILLE HWY. Two-story pioneer log house and out-buildings, some reconstructed, where North Carolina's Civil War governor was born. Visitor's center. Spring and fall, artisans in period costume demonstrate early craft making, such as quilting and wood-working. Mon–Sat, 9–5; Sun, 1–5. (704) 645-6706

15 **Mostrom & Chase** 128 BLACKBERRY INN RD. GO TO END OF REEMS CREEK, LEFT AT "T" INTERSECTION, then immediately right on Blackberry Inn Rd, house on left. Traditional loom weaving includes the Double Bowknot pattern. In 1895, Francis Goodrich received the gift of a coverlet in this pattern, vegetable-dyed and perfectly woven, moving her to found Allanstand Cottage Indus-

The Road Goes On Forever
Side Trips, adventures, and treasure hunts

tries. These heritage pieces will move you, too. Mon–Fri, 1–5. (704) 658-9274

 Kathy Triplett GO BACK DOWN BLACKBERRY INN RD, MAKING RIGHT AT THE STONE CHURCH ONTO MCDARIS COVE RD (#175), 1.8 miles on steep, ornery gravel road to the end. Teapots, sconces, change banks, tiles, wall sculptures, architectural details. From clay, this woman creates a joyous deco wonderland. Thurs–Fri, 12–4. (704) 658-3207

SPUR TO BARNARDSVILLE

From Kathy Triplett's, return to Blackberry Inn Rd. and turn right. At Maney (Paint Fork) Road, turn right again. Take this combination paved and gravel road 5.6 miles up and over the mountain into Barnardsville.

 Rocky Creek Farm Studio 12 SPRUCE ST. FROM PAINT FORK RD TURN RIGHT ON 197, go one block, turn right at the Baptist Church onto Spruce. Road forks, take right branch. Dried florals, pottery, jewelry, dolls, baskets. Fri–Sat, 10–5 (Mar–Dec). (704) 626-3187

The Hawk & Ivy B&B RETURN TO HWY 197 AND TURN RIGHT. GO 1/2 MILE TO #133. Comfortable farm house with two-story guest cottage and gift shop, near a national forest and the Ivy River. The innkeeper's expanding garden provides fresh berries, fruits and flowers for your table. (704) 626-3486

To find Weaverville from Barnardsville, take Hwy 197 W to 19/23, turning off into Weaverville (Exit 25-70).

IN WEAVERVILLE

Secret Garden IN THE MAYOR'S OLD HOUSE, 56 N. MAIN ST. Turn right onto Main from Weaver Blvd (US 25/70). Enclosed wrap-around porch makes private sitting rooms for each first floor bedroom. Make reservations for Christmas; the decorations are straight out of *House Beautiful* and each guest gets a personal gift. (704) 658-9317

Handles of polished laurel top off Nancy Fargo's pottery.

Bob Wager's oil lamps.

LIKE A TUMBLIN' TUMBLEWEED
William S. Hart served as Asheville's first professional community theater director before becoming a star of westerns in Hollywood.

Guidebook Symbols

🤚	Craft Studio	🍴	Restaurant
🔵	Craft Gallery	🏠	Lodging
🔴	Historic Site	⭐	Special Attraction

Top: Upstairs at Grovewood Gallery.

Bottom: Fred Weisner's pottery is worth smiling about.

20 **4 Cent Cotton Cafe** 18 N. MAIN ST, WEAVERVILLE. Continental American cuisine, homemade deserts. Louisiana natives must try the gumbo; it will remind you of home. Ask a member of the wait staff about the quaint name of this convenient eatery. It has something to do with the depression, prohibition, and an old song. Tues–Sat, 11:30–10, Sun, 11–3. (704) 658-2660

21 **Dry Ridge Inn** 26 BROWN ST. TAKE MAIN TO S. MAIN, TURN RIGHT ON BROWN ST. Built in 1849 as a parsonage for a nearby revival campground. Today it's a welcome sanctuary. Innkeepers Paul and Mary Lou Gibson have installed a baby grand in the parlor and a gourmet cook in the kitchen. Seven rooms. (704) 658-3899

22 **Gourmet Gardens Herb Farm** 14 BANKS TOWN RD. TURN RIGHT OFF MAIN ST. TO HWY 19, LEFT ON BANKS TOWN RD. (opposite Lake Louise). The "grow-god" hovers over this fine rock herb garden. Inside, extravagant natural wreaths confirm the expertise of your host, who is also the author of some handsome books you may browse. Tues–Sat, 9:30–5:30 (Mar–Nov). (704) 658-0766

DOWNTOWN ASHEVILLE

Take 19/23 to 240 East. Exit at Charlotte St., turn left, and follow signs to Grove Park Inn.

23 **Grove Park Inn** 290 MACON AVE. Conceived by E.W. Grove, and brought to reality by his son-in-law Fred Seely who constructed it in 11 months from blueprints in his head. The Inn has expanded since then, but it remains a tribute to arts and crafts style. Its original custom-built furniture and hand-hammered copper lighting fixtures came from the Roycroft crafters of New York. Over 500 rooms. (704) 252-2711

24 **Gallery of the Mountains** VANDERBILT WING, GROVE PARK INN. You will find larger collections of craft elsewhere, but none finer. Hand dyed and hand painted silk vests, handwoven coats, wraps, and scarves, pottery, jewelry, and woodwork, all assembled and displayed with considerable verve. Sun–Tues, 9–6; Wed–Sat, 9–9 (704) 254-2068

25 **Grovewood Cafe** 111 GROVEWOOD RD., ADJACENT TO GROVE PARK INN. English cottage set among lofty evergreens. Idyllic setting for a romantic lunch or for getting reacquainted with an old friend at dinner. The food just happens to be fabulous, too. (704) 258-8956

The Road Goes On Forever
Side Trips, adventures, and treasure hunts

A WELLSPRING OF A CITY
Thomas Wolfe wrote about Asheville, of course, and he changed the course of other writer's lives. James Jones came here to live and find something of the spirit of Wolfe before writing **From Here To Eternity** *.*

26 **Grovewood Gallery** 111 GROVEWOOD RD. Two floors of furniture, glass, pottery, clothing and jewelry confirm your suspicion that you have, indeed, reached an epicenter of ground-breaking work. Inquire here about Grovewood Studios, home to artists represented by the Gallery who gladly do custom work on request. Mon–Sat, 10–6; Sun, 1–5. (704) 253-7651

Return to downtown Asheville via Charlotte St. and College St. Asheville has attractive and safe parking facilities on Rankin Ave., Otis St., and behind the Civic Center. From these locations, you can walk to any of the following:

27 **T. S. Morrison's** 39 LEXINGTON AVE. Asheville's oldest store and emporium. Handmade baskets and train whistles. Wooden toys from Berea College. And a cache of sweeter merchandise: Licorice pulls, atomic fireballs, taffy, bon bons, peppermint puffs, pecan turtles, Wilbur buds, rock candy, and jelly beans. Mon–Sat, 10–6. (704) 253-2348

28 **Blue Dog Art** 34 LEXINGTON AVE. Crafts that create friendly whispers, sly smiles, and muffled giggles. All fun stuff. Many different media. Mon–Sat, 11–6; Sun, 12–5 (704) 258-3586

29 **Turtle Creek** 24 WALL ST. Native American designs by Steve Ricker expressed in dream catchers, furniture, and ceremonial hangings. Mon–Wed, 9–5; Thurs–Sat, 10–9. (704) 259-9252

30 **Beads and Beyond** 35 WALL ST. Classes in beading, leathercraft. Handcrafted local jewelry. Native American craft. Mon–Wed, 11–6; Thurs, 11–8; Fri–Sat, 11–9; Sun, 1–4. (704) 254-7927

31 **Jewelry Design** 63 HAYWOOD ST. Three talented jewelry designers practice this glistening art; one of them, Paula Dawkins, recently named as one of the 12 top new designers in the nation. Mon–Sat, 10–6. (704) 254-5088

32 **Earth Guild** 33 HAYWOOD ST. Looms at the ready for lessons. Bins of many colored yarns and supplies for all sorts of fiber arts. Mon–Sat, 10–6. (704) 255-7818

33 **Mother Earth Trading Post & Gallery** 46 HAYWOOD ST. IN THE HAYWOOD PARK HOTEL ATRIUM. Northern Plains Indian reproduction bead work, leather work and other pieces. Tues–Sat, 10–5. (704) 285-0509

34 **Appalachian Craft Center** 10 NORTH SPRUCE ST. Old time mountain crafts. Handcrafted brooms, face jugs, looper rugs, Garrou pottery, fan pulls and

THE URBAN TRAIL: A PATHWAY THROUGH TIME

A delicious way to befriend the history of this unique city, especially Asheville's boom period between 1880 and 1930. All it takes is a comfortable pair of walking shoes, a curious mind, and the Urban Trail guide to 27 stops. (Guide available at Pack Place and other downtown locations.) Over 1.6 miles, you will visit an era of flamboyance that included the stylings of writers O. Henry, Fitzgerald and Thomas Wolfe, the architecture of Raphael Guastavino and Douglas Ellington, and the enduring legacies of George Willis Pack and E. W. Grove.

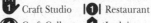

Sweeping beauty. Brooms by Kim English.

Out of reach: a work exhibited at The Chair Show, organized by the Southern Highland Craft Guild. The chairmaker is Jake Cress.

clay creatures. Mon–Sat, 10–5. (704) 253-8499

35 Thomas Wolfe House Memorial 48 SPRUCE ST. The boarding house which sits, full of life and conversation, in the pages of *Look Homeward Angel*. If nothing else, merge with a rocking chair on the front porch and listen to the people come and go in 1920. Nearby, at 67 Market, you're welcome to drop by the HandMade in America office anytime during the week (9 to 5) just to say hello or get directions. (704) 253-8304

36 Pack Place Education, Arts, & Science Center TWO SOUTH PACK SQ. A gem-like, multi-faceted cultural center for the mountain region that keeps getting better. Always something going on—an exhibit, a juried show, a performance—that instructs the heart and stretches the imagination. Adults $3.00–$5.50. (The Urban Trail starts here.) Tues–Sat, 10–5 (Year-round); Sun, 1–5 (June–Oct). (704) 257-4500

37 Blue Spiral Gallery 38 BILTMORE AVE. Against its white walls and upon its plain and simple pedestals, there is a whirling dervish of art here, with frequent new shows. If an artist or craftsperson has work at Blue Spiral, somewhere, somehow he or she has pushed the edge of something rather amazing and wonderful. A must: the permanent collection of oils and pastels by artist Will Henry Stevens (1881-1949). Mon–Sat, 10–5. (704) 251-0202

38 Stebo BEHIND HOT DOG KING, OFF BILTMORE AVE. Strange things happen to environmental castaways in a studio overrun by stacked-up green frogs and garden creatures, all of which have leapt full-blown from Stefan Bonitz's imagination. Mon–Fri, 12–4. (704) 274-5492

39 Blue Moon Bakery 60 BILTMORE AVE. The particular combination of hearth-baked bread, coffee, and conversation around cafe tables makes this one of the most soulful places in Asheville (or anywhere else in the modern world). Mon–Fri, 7:30–6; Sat, 9–5. (704) 252-6063

ASHEVILLE INNS AND B&B'S

There are an abundance of historic, captivating inns in the Asheville area.

Space limitations prevent a full, descriptive accounting in this book; however a complete list is available at the Visitor's Center of the Asheville Area Chamber of Commerce. The following is simply a starting point for discovering inns of note.

The Road Goes On Forever
Side Trips, adventures, and treasure hunts

Julia Wolfe's "Old Kentucky Home," the boarding house in her novelist son's stories of "Altamont," no longer operates but you can visit the place anyway (see listing under "Asheville"). No matter which inn you settle on, be sure to call ahead.

Richmond Hill.

The Black Walnut B & B Inn 288 MONTFORD AVE. (704) 254-3878

Blake House 150 ROYAL PINES DRIVE, ARDEN. (704) 684-1847

Cedar Crest 674 BILTMORE AVENUE. National Register of Historic Places. (704) 252-1389

Flint Street Inns B & B 100 & 116 FLINT ST. (704) 253-6723

The Inn on Montford 296 MONTFORD AVE. (704) 254-9569

The Old Reynolds Mansion 100 REYNOLDS HEIGHTS. (704) 254-0496

Richmond Hill Inn 87 RICHMOND HILL DRIVE. National Register of Historic Places. (704) 252-7313

The Wright Inn 235 PEARSON DRIVE. (704) 251-0789

Beyond Grits

True, you can find plain grits, fried grits, buttered grits, and cheese grits without much trouble. But the larger question is, what else is there? The restaurants listed below offer up a tantalizing answer—each serving regional (and other) cuisine in its own heartfelt way. Within this list, and at other exceptional dining establishments in and near Asheville, you will discover some of the most wonderful food this side of New York City.

Cafe On The Square ONE BILTMORE AVE. High-ceilinged, white-tableclothed space that smiles and sparkles with fine service on a busy corner. (704) 251-5565

The Marketplace 20 WALL STREET. Chef Mark Rosenstein has turned this place into an institution of joyous chopping, sautéing, filleting, and general celebration. He's totally, and unredeemably, mad about food. (704) 252-4162

Pisgah View Ranch Platters heaped with apples, sweet potatoes, cornbread, cobblers and other amazements of this life, served family-style. (704) 667-9100

Richmond Hill Inn 87 RICHMOND HILL DR. In

Guidebook Symbols

 Craft Studio    Restaurant

Craft Gallery   Lodging

Historic Site   Special Attraction

Top: Stan Flote's "Juggernaut"

Bottom: Looking into Judy Weilbacher's glass.

this architectural treasure lies a restaurant of surprising consequence. (704) 252-7313

Terrace Restaurant GROVE PARK INN, 290 MACON AVE. If the view and the food don't stir you, you may want to check your pulse. (704) 252-2711

23 Page Restaurant at Haywood Park Hotel ONE BATTERY PARK AVE. This tasteful address offers a worldly, sweet sophistication and dinners that match. For lighter fare, The New French Bar streetside, upstairs. (704) 252-3685

ASHEVILLE SIDETRIPS

(40) Touch of Glass 421 HAYWOOD RD. Stained glass for your Christmas tree, your memorial window or your achievement plaque. Mon–Fri, 10:30–5; Sat, 10:30–3. (704) 258-2749

(41) Odyssey Center for the Ceramic Arts 236 CLINGMAN AVE. An adjunct of Highwater Clay, one of the leading suppliers of clay for professionals in the Southeast. Director Mark Burleson and resident potters teach nine-week pottery classes. Celebrated guest potters also appear for weekend workshops. For more information call, or better yet, drop by and meet this friendly, talented bunch of folks. Mon–Thurs, 12–6; Fri, 9–5; Sat–Sun, 11–3. (704) 252-6033

(42) W.N.C. Farmers Market 570 BREVARD RD. Bushels and pecks of everything. Peaches, tomatoes, corn, pumpkins, flowers, cabbage, oranges, grapefruit, sourwood honey, crafts from the farm, and

An endearing high chair by Lothlorien's Mike Hester.

"I Built a House of Ice Water and Autumn Leaves" by Mary B. White.

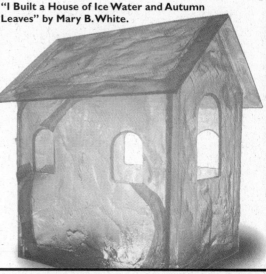

The Road Goes On Forever

Side Trips, adventures, and treasure hunts

In 1934, Chimney Rock hired Douglas Ellington, architect of Asheville's City Building, to oversee projects at the park. True to his way of seeing things, Ellington insisted on preserving natural lichens and mosses on nearby rocks so new buildings would blend into their natural setting.

an extensive nursery. The whole place gets up with the sun. (Truck sheds open at 7.) Seven days, 8–5. (704) 253-1691

👋 **43 Kayne & Son Custom Hardware** 100 DANIEL RIDGE RD. TAKE SMOKY PARK HIGHWAY TO ENKA, TURN RIGHT ON ASBURY. Turn left on Monte Vista, then right on Daniel Ridge Rd. Accomplished ironwork for home or castle. In the latter category, Kayne has replaced door hinges and other hardware at Biltmore House. Mon–Fri, 8:30–5:30. (704) 667-8868

BILTMORE VILLAGE

👋 **44 Lothlorien** 244-B SWANNANOA RIVER RD. When we visited, a master woodworker here was carving a lifesize St. Francis of Assisi from maple. By now, it graces the church that commissioned it. But stop by anyway. These two talented craftspeople are always up to their elbows in wood. Mon–Fri, 8:30– 5:30. (704) 258-1445

St. Francis emerging from maple. Carved by Mark Strom.

45 Vitrum 10 LODGE ST. If you have ever wondered why North Carolina has a worldwide reputation for its glass, step inside this evocative, light-filled space. Tues–Sat, 11–5. (704) 274-9900

46 Hot Shot Cafe 7 LODGE ST. We're not positive, but we think you have to have a beehive hairdo to be a waitress here. Breakfast (anytime), lunch, and dinner served up in 50's style. Featured in *The New York Times*. (704) 274-2170

Robert Stephan's "It's Plain to See."

47 Legacies 2 BOSTON WAY. In summer, cool off with backyard ice cream. Inside, wood carvings, handmade miniatures, candles, and copper fountains, many pieces crafted by the owners. Mon–Sat, 10– 5. (704) 274-8212

👋 **48 Early Music Shop** 3 BILTMORE PLAZA. Dulcimers, strumsticks, flutes, drums, psalteries, ocarinas, kalimbas, and other charmed and noteworthy instruments in an enchanting corner shop. Mon– Sat, 10–5:30. (704) 274-2890

49 Bellagio CORNER BOSTON WAY AND BILTMORE PLAZA. Museum-quality clothes, jewelry, and accessories. Paris and Milan filtered through the Appalachians. Mon–Sat, 10–6; Sun, 12–5. (704) 277-8100

50 New Morning Gallery 7 BOSTON WAY. The "gallery at the top of the stairs" that remains as fresh and alluring as the day John Cram opened it some 20 years ago. Along with an unerring eye, John has the uncanny ability to craft spaces as endear-

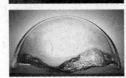

"MountainSkyscape' by Marc Peiser.

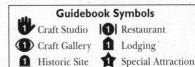

Guidebook Symbols

👋 Craft Studio   🍴 Restaurant

🏺 Craft Gallery   🏠 Lodging

🏛 Historic Site   ⭐ Special Attraction

Sugars, creamers, and cups at Pisgah Forest Pottery and the bell out front.

ing as the work they hold. Simply the best in pottery, metal, jewelry, wood, textiles. Mon–Sat, 10–6; Sun, 12–5. (704) 274-2831

(51) Village Galleries 32 ALL SOULS CRESCENT. Another reason craft-seekers hold Biltmore Village in such esteem. A spritely and varied collection. Pay particular attention to the hand-blown glass, the dolls and the quilts. Mon–Fri, 10–5; Sat, 11–4. (704) 274-2424

(52) Biltmore Estate WITH ENTRANCE ON HWY 25A IN BILTMORE VILLAGE. George and Edith Vanderbilt's quaint 255-room French chateau built in 1895 by the architectural dandy of the time, William Morris Hunt. The most prominent and successful, self-supporting historical property in America. Whether you are wandering the great rooms of this place or Frederick Law Olmsted's vast and beautiful grounds, prepare yourself for a totally exhilarating experience. Winery, gardens, restaurants, cafes, retail shops, and more architectural detailing than you are ever likely to see in one place in your entire life. Admission: Adults, $24.95. Year-round. (800) 543-2961

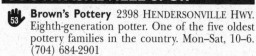

SOUTH ASHEVILLE SPUR

(53) Brown's Pottery 2398 HENDERSONVILLE HWY. Eighth-generation potter. One of the five oldest pottery families in the country. Mon–Sat, 10–6. (704) 684-2901

(54) Mountain Rug Mills 6385 HENDERSONVILLE HWY, FLETCHER. Handmade hooked rugs and Early American braided rugs. Choose from traditional designs or your own dreamscape. Mon–Fri, 9–5. (704) 684-7131

ON 191 TO HENDERSONVILLE

From Biltmore Village, drive south on US 25 (Hendersonville Rd.), turn right onto the Blue Ridge Parkway, crossing the French Broad River. At the river, swing off to the right onto NC 191.

(55) NC Arboretum NORTH ON 191 TO BENT CREEK RANCH RD—THE SIGNS WILL LEAD YOU. A developing 426-acre facility of national bearing which is a member of the University of North Carolina system. You may explore a bounty of trails and gardens, including (appropriately for our purposes) the Appalachian Quilt Garden. Also handcrafted wrought iron gates in the Stream and Spring Gardens. There are many natural wonders; the best is the effect this place has on human beings. Mon–

The Road Goes On Forever

Side Trips, adventures, and treasure hunts

HOME IN FLAT ROCK
After roaming and writing about the whole of America, Carl Sandburg set his orange crates and typewriter down at Connemara. "There is only one man in the world," he wrote, "and his name is All Men."

Fri, 9–5; second and fourth Sun, 1:30–4:30; Sat (after July 1996), 9–5. (704) 665-2492

(56) Evan's Pottery FROM NC 191 TURN LEFT ONTO CLAYTON RD. A storehouse of everyday, functional pottery, including large patio urns, some dappled. Also fluted dishes and face jugs. Mon–Sat, 9–5 (April–Dec). (704) 684-6842

Painted furniture by Joe Bruneau at Touchstone.

(57) Pisgah Forest Pottery TO THE LEFT IN A GLEN WITH A BROOK JUST OFF 191. Established by Walter Stephen in 1926, this charming collection of small buildings is practically a national shrine to pottery-making. In its tiny free-standing gift shop, you will find dinnerware and comfortable mugs long famous for their turquoise, wine, jade, and crystalline glazes. The folks here mix their own clay on the property and fire up a kiln stoked with pine wood. Mon–Sat, 9 to 5 (May–Oct). (704) 684-6663

(58) Candlertown Chairworks 14 BOYLSTON HWY, MILLS RIVER. Turn left. Stone and brick building exactly one mile down on left. Ladderbacks, armchairs, barstools, and other two and three syllable chair types. All handcrafted in traditional ways. Mon–Fri, 9–5. (704) 891-1010

(59) BernWell Pottery TO THE LEFT ON 191, 2.7 MILES NORTH OF HENDERSONVILLE CITY LIMITS. Four hands at work: hers creating practical, yet beautiful, dinnerware; his crafting more dramatic pieces for preparing and presenting foods. Tues–Sat, 10–5. (704) 693-8229.

IN HENDERSONVILLE

(60) Sweet Memories 430 MAIN ST. One of the most expansive displays of pottery in the region, ranging from traditional to contemporary. Mon–Sat, 10–5:30. (704) 692-8401

(61) Brightwater Art Glass 342 N. MAIN ST. Leaded, stained and etched glass for windows, skylights, transoms and such. Seven days. Mon–Sat, 9–5; Sun, 1–5. (704) 697-6842

(62) Touchstone Gallery 318 N. MAIN ST. Beautifully selected, ofttimes whimsical, art and craft created by contemporary American artists. A gonzo-gift-giving-kind-of-place where you'll find work of enchantment for any age. Mon–Sat, 9:30–6, Sun, 12–5. (704) 692-2191

(63) Hendersonville Curb Market 2ND AVE. AND CHURCH ST. Flowers, preserved foods, fresh cakes, woven goods and wood carvings. Tues, Thurs, Sat, 8–2.

Guidebook Symbols

🖐	Craft Studio	🍴	Restaurant
①	Craft Gallery	🛏	Lodging
①	Historic Site	⭐	Special Attraction

St. John in the Wilderness.

At the Woodfield.

(64) Four Seasons Crafters 475 S. CHURCH ST. Fifty-member co-op offering array of cottage crafts. Mon–Sat, 9–6; Sun, 1–6. (704) 698-0016

(65) Bonesteel's Hardware and Quilt Corner 150 WHITE ST. Yes, you've seen Georgia on TV. A dynamite stop for any quilter: fabric, patterns, classes, hardware, along with machines for stitching and quilting. Mon–Sat, 8–5:30. (704) 692-0293

(66) Cottage Crafts 121 STATON AVE. A store that preserves the tradition and skill of hearthside crafts. Local artists. Mon–Fri, 10–6. (704) 692-0082

|67| The Poplar Lodge 2350 HEBRON ROAD. Three miles from downtown Hendersonville (call for directions). Once an inn, now a beacon for patrons of fine dining and lovers of life, in general. Roaring fireplaces in winter; mountain breezes in summer. Beef aged on the premises and cut to preference. Year-round. Mon–Sat, 6–10; Sun, 4–8. (704) 692-9191

I-26 EXCURSION

(68) A Day in the Country 130 SUGARLOAF RD. A showroom for joined and woven craft from The Manual Woodworkers & Weavers in Gerton (see listing later). Mon–Sat, 9–9; Sun, 11–6. (704) 692-7914

(69) Country Village Crafts OFF I-26 AT UPWARD RD. Cottage crafts. Mon-Sat, 10-5 (704) 693-8284

FLAT ROCK

US 25 south will take you into Flat Rock.

|70| Highland Lake HIGHLAND LAKE RD IN FLAT ROCK. Gourmet (homegrown) cuisine, gardens, greenhouses, critters and barns. Combining the up-to-date with the gentle elements of times gone by. Sunday brunch, Wednesday buffet. (704) 693-6812

71 St. John in the Wilderness US 25, ¾ OF A MILE NORTH OF CARL SANDBURG HISTORIC SHRINE. Built in 1833 as the chapel for a country estate. It later became the first Episcopal church in Western North Carolina. Some 10 years before Lincoln's Emancipation Proclamation, slaves and white families worshipped side by side in the church's pews.

72 Carl Sandburg Home National Historic Site OFF US 25 S AT FLAT ROCK PLAYHOUSE. The home of Carl Sandburg during his later years. The house is built in low-country plantation style. Books and

---

The Road Goes On Forever
Side Trips, adventures, and treasure hunts

They're loud, they're rambunctious, they'll never win a beauty contest—and they're celebrities! At Coon Dog Days, every July in Saluda.

memorabilia. Through the week, 9–5, except Christmas. A fee of $2 for house tour. (704) 693-4178

 73 **David Voorhees, potter; Molly Sharp, jeweler and metalsmith** 1850 GREENVILLE HWY, FLAT ROCK. David creates elegant decorative porcelain reminiscent of a garden path; Molly works with silver, gold, brass, and copper pieces to create evocative rings, earrings and other designs. Mon–Sat, 9–5. (704) 697-7719

74 **Woodfield Inn** US 25 AT FLAT ROCK. North Carolina's oldest inn in continuous operation. Antebellum dining rooms. Meals to please those hailing from either side of the Mason-Dixon line. (704) 693-6016

SALUDA

From Flat Rock, pick up US 176 to Saluda.

One of Kathy Triplett's hip tea pots.

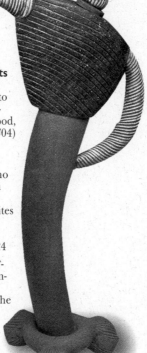

75 **Shady Lane** MAIN ST. A scrumptious destination, beginning with the coffee and baked goods up front. Some totally heart-warming, alluring work by Penland graduates and others, many of whom have chosen Saluda as home. A number of potters, a bookmaker, an iron-worker, and a photographer are among artists represented. (704) 749-1155

76 **Heartwood Contemporary Crafts Gallery** MAIN ST. Versatile "chair" hammocks made on site in colors to fit the porch, the kitchen, the bedroom, or your mood. Tempting wood, pottery, jewelry. Mon–Sat, 10–5. (704) 749-9365

77 **Wildflour Bakery** NOSTALGIA COURTYARD, MAIN ST. Bread has no preservatives, but don't worry. You will eat the whole loaf before you leave the parking lot. Lunch favorites include pocket veggie sandwiches that look like old fashioned apple jacks. Wed–Sat, 8–4. (704) 749-9224

78 **Stormy Knob** NOSTALGIA COURTYARD, MAIN ST. A potter whose contemporary work mimics the movement and colors of nature. The gallery includes jewelry, glass, and wood by other artisans. Tues–Sat, 10–5. (704) 749-1370

Guidebook Symbols

🖐 **1** Craft Studio		🍽 **1** Restaurant
⬤ **1** Craft Gallery		🏠 **1** Lodging
■ **1** Historic Site		⭐ **1** Special Attraction

At the Esmerelda.

A victorian lady in Bat Cave.

(79) Marie's Web NOSTALGIA COURTYARD, MAIN ST. Hand-painted furniture and decorative painting, including faux stone/marble work. Mon–Sat, 10–5. (704) 894-2286

(80) ArtaCloaks NOSTALGIA COURTYARD, DOWN-STAIRS. Hand-dyed vests and jackets with abstract paintings meant to be worn but suitable for framing. Mother and daughter artists team with Tallfeather Woodworks in a very spiffy gallery. Wed–Sat, 10–5. (704) 749-1162

(81) The Wood Shed NOSTALGIA COURTYARD, MAIN ST. Shopkeepers paint critters while you browse this wee shop of wooden items and hand-woven rugs. Wed–Sat, 10–5; Sun, 1–5. (704) 749-7711

(82) Acme Anvil Art NEXT DOOR TO THE WOOD SHED. Sculpts and forges table bases and various and sundry other decorative pieces. Tues–Sat, 10–5. (704) 859-5063

(83) French Broad River Decoy Company AT EXIT 28, I-26. Largest manufacturer of decoys in N.C. They are turned in the shop and finished by hand. Also blanket and steamer chests. Mon–Sat, 10–5, Sun 1–5. (704) 749-9543

(84) Saluda Mountain Craft Gallery OZONE DR. AT EXIT 28, I-26. Wood, pottery, quilts and jewelry from local and regional artists. Follow your instincts to the fine furniture upstairs and the fine fudge next door. Tues–Sat, 10–6, Sun 11–6. (704) 749-4341

(85) The Orchard Inn ONE MILE SOUTH OF SALUDA ON 176. The prototype for an inn Norman Rockwell might paint with Early Americana throughout—in furnishings, bric-a-brac, table settings, and the cordiality of drawing rooms. There's a friendliness about that belies description, and it's worth the drive from Saluda, or Alaska, to get here. (800) 581-3800

Continue on 176 into Tryon.

TRYON

(86) Fig Falls 1458 HWY 176N. Owner is potter/weaver. Wheel-thrown and hand-built pottery. Hand woven rugs. Seven days, 9–5. (704) 859-5285.

(87) Tryon Crafts, Inc. 208 MELROSE AVE., ABOVE FINE ARTS CENTER. Offering instruction in a wide variety of crafts including needlework, knitting, lapidary work, early American decoration, enameling, stained glass, pottery, chair caning and quilting. Mon–Fri, 9–12. (704) 859-8323

The Road Goes On Forever
Side Trips, adventures, and treasure hunts

TURN OF PHRASE
"A Motor Trip Veritably to Nature's Heart in 'Land of the Sky,'" announced a brochure about the mountains in 1919.

88 **Pine Crest Inn** 200 PINE CREST LN. Built in 1900 and converted to an equestrian retreat in 1917. Fitzgerald and Hemingway stayed here. Closed January. (800) 633-3001

89 **Hand Painted Tiles** 216 BROADWAY. The tiles are beautiful. A two-person shop with most work on contract for interior designers. In collaboration with Acme Anvil Art in Saluda, they make occasional tables that are full of color and life. Tues–Sat, 10–5. (704) 859-8316

90 **Tryon House** 220 N TRADE ST. Crafts and gifts. Town mascot Morris hangs out here, in every imaginable incarnation, including the original—as a toy horse. Mon–Sat, 9:30–5. (704) 859-9962

91 **Mimosa Inn** ONE MIMOSA LN. Situated on the site of the Mills Plantation. A stop for travelers for 200 years. Rebuilt in 1916 after a fire destroyed the original. Nine rooms. (704) 859-7688

92 **Mills-Mosseller** 1205 LYNN RD. In sanctuary of 1914 church. Limited parking on upper road. Hand-hooked rugs of considerable merit. Sales by commission only, once for the Little White House in Georgia when the Roosevelts were there. Second generation. (704) 859-5336

Along the way.

COLUMBUS

From Tryon, take NC 108 to Columbus.

93 **Little Mountain Pottery** SIX MILES FROM COLUMBUS ON PENIEL RD. A country pottery with shop and showroom. Mon–Sat, 10–4. (704) 894-8091

94 **The Gnome Workshop** 798 HWY 108 PEA RIDGE. (FOUR MILES EAST OF MILL SPRING, NC.) Aromas from the apple-cinnamon bread can stop, or start, a war. The work of local artists and craftsmen competes for attention with cakes and pies. Tues–Sat, 10–5. (704) 894-8558

NEAR LAKE LURE

Take Hwy 9 north to Lake Lure, turning right on US 64/74 to AppleValleyFarm.

95 **Apple Valley Farm/The Apple Seed Shop** FOLLOW HWY 64/74 TO BILLS CREEK RD., DRIVE TWO MILES, THEN LEFT ON BUFFALO CREEK RD. A 300-acre farm shaping itself into a lush center for craft production and sales. Area quilts, pottery and Mennonite furniture. Mon–Sat, 10–5; Sun, 12:30–5. (704) 625-1999

Return to Lake Lure via Hwy 64/74A.

Guidebook Symbols

 Craft Studio  Restaurant

Craft Gallery Lodging

Historic Site Special Attraction

On the lake at the Lodge at Lake Lure.

Elegant as ever: the Lake Lure Inn.

LAKE LURE

96 **The Lodge at Lake Lure** Among other delights, there's a windowed, rim porch above the lake where, if you blink twice, you could easily confuse your view with Banff or some lakescape in Northern Italy. A boathouse below for departures by single canoe, motored ensemble, or flotilla. (704) 625-2789

97 **Point of View Restaurant** SHORELINE OF LAKE LURE AT THE OLD MARINA. Check the time of sunset before you make a reservation. Ask for a window seat. The timeless beauty of the lake will steer your appetite towards trout or something more exotic on the menu. Dinner only. (704) 625-4380

98 **Lake Lure Inn** AT THE BEACH. Still as elegant as it must have been when Franklin D. Roosevelt, F. Scott Fitzgerald and Emily Post took refuge here. Restored with Victorian furnishings and 20s panache. Year round, dinner only. Closed Mon. Brunch only on Sun., 11–2. Reservations suggested. (704) 625-2525

99 **Red Barn & Bear Company** BEHIND THE LAKE LURE INN. Old barn that once served as a community building now houses a community of craft, collectibles, food and music. Try the kudzu jelly, warm by the fireplace at Mimi's and examine the dulcimers at Smoky Mountain Dulcimers. It's a given you'll find something amusing here. Red Barn, year round, 8:30–5. (704) 625-0204. Mimi's Tea Room, 9–3. (704) 625-8327. Smoky Mountain Dulcimer, 8:30–5. (704) 625-0907

100 **Chimney Rock Park** HWY 64/74A, CHIMNEY ROCK. An early advertisement called it "the most stupendously interesting scenic objective in the South." Today's promotional material is a bit more understated, but the park is no less alluring in its

Past lives; the pottery of Don Davis.

The Road Goes On Forever

Side Trips, adventures, and treasure hunts

"The railway train, thundering under the very walls of the Balsams and climbing across them through the high Balsam Gap, bespeaks a new era when people come in throngs to the mountains for other purposes than bear hunting."
Margaret Morley, *The Carolina Mountains* (1913)

natural drama. In fact, you may have already been there if you've seen the film "Last of the Mohicans." Almost a thousand acres, including cliff and forest trails, 400-foot Hickory Nut Falls, and overlooks of considerable magic. Adult admission: $6.00, Dec 1 to April 1; $9.50, rest of year. (800) 277-9611

Esmerelda Inn & Restaurant HWY 64/74A, CHIMNEY ROCK. Make this your own private hideaway; the movie stars have. Clark Gable, Gloria Swanson, Douglas Fairbanks and Mary Pickford used Esmeralda as a place to refresh themselves. Lunch and dinner daily. Sunday dinner, 4–8 (April–mid-Nov). Reservations recommended. (704) 625-9105

...or just whistle.

A Touch in Time HWY 64/74A, BAT CAVE. A variety of craft objects spill out onto the porch of this 1902 Victorian on the hill. Through the week, 10:30–5 (June–Oct). Weekends only (April–May). (704) 625-1902

The Manual Woodworkers & Weavers IN GERTON ON US 74, TOWARDS ASHEVILLE. A bit of a North Pole workshop gone south with wooden and woven pieces most everywhere you turn. Mon–Sat, 9–9; Sun, 1–6. (704) 692-7914

Return to Asheville (and the Parkway) via US 74 or scoot up Hwy 9 from Bat Cave, taking the "Black Mountain Rag," a lush and twisty scenic byway that intersects with I-40. Return to Asheville following this interstate.

Black Mountain Rag

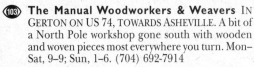

A Fairview stopping place in the fall of the year.

Named for the musical form, this byway loops, dips and swirls in the same jaunty fashion. In its Black Mountain to Bat Cave section, you'll be hard-pressed to find a flat spot or a straight stretch that lasts more than a millisecond. On the other hand, it's the quintessential mountain road. Before turning north, this byway offers up some wonderful views of Lake Lure with its sentinal-like cliffs and bluffs. Owners of recreational vehicles may want to avoid the steep upper section of Route 9.

Guidebook Symbols

	Craft Studio		Restaurant
	Craft Gallery		Lodging
	Historic Site		Special Attraction

Biltmore and Craft
An Artfull Industry

When Mr. George Vanderbilt and his architect, Richard Morris Hunt determined to build a European chateau, it quickly became apparent that they would need European craftspeople to do the work. In all, there were over 1,000 individuals who contributed to the actual building of the great house, including stone-cutters, woodworkers, masons, sculptors, carvers, carpenters, tile-makers, glaziers, blacksmiths, painters, and their apprentices. They traveled into the mountains from faraway places – from England, Spain, Italy, France, Ireland, Austria – and from European neighborhoods and enclaves in New York and Philadelphia.

Many stayed well beyond the five years it took to craft Biltmore House. They stayed to work on an even larger canvas – the cityscape of Asheville, a mountain town which had, in the meantime, quadrupled in size and become a magnet for tourists of every station. Their contributions live on in architecture, public and private; in bungalows, in cathedrals, in city buildings, in streetscapes, stone carvings, and iron-work.

Edith and Cornelia Vanderbuilt.

It took five years and hundreds of workers to complete the Biltmore House.

Biltmore Industries.

In the midst of this turn-of-the-century boom period, a quiet renaissance began to emerge in silviculture and native handcraft due, once again, to the sweeping stewardship of George and Edith Vanderbilt. For while George organized the first forestry school in America, Edith organized Biltmore Industries, a training school for young men and women in mountain crafts—particularly wood carving and the weaving of woolen homespun cloth.

The industry continued, moved from Biltmore Village to the grounds of Grove Park Inn, for nearly 70 years. During its heyday, when 40 looms clapped in sliding rhythm, the products of the business spun an international reputation. Colorfully dyed bolts of woolen cloth became wastecoats and jackets, some warming the shoulders of ambassadors and presidents. One particular dye, in fact, earned the name "Coolidge Red."

In the early eighties, these looms ceased their artful industry. But the mountain craft renaissance ignited by the Vanderbilts continues to light a path for contemporary artists and their devoted followers.

Cascades Trail

Water is a constant, reassuring presence on the Cascades Trail. It tumbles, trickles, courses, and pools all along this breathtaking route.))) At the start, Hwy 276 and the Davidson River are woven together as neatly as a schoolgirl's braid. Crisscrossing back and forth through Pisgah National Forest, they chase each other all the way to the outskirts of Brevard.))) In the summer months, this picturesque town plays host to hundreds of music students from around the world, and thousands of visitors who come to see them perform at the renowned Brevard Music Center.))) Going toward Cedar Mountain, the French Broad River takes up where the Davidson left off, accompanying you to a virtual potter's row of notable galleries and studio spaces. It's here, in the wet clay, in the buckets of liquid glaze, that one realizes how water is just as elemental to a turned pot or vase as it is to each of us.))) The road to the resort communi-

Summer campers make faces at John Dodson's Mud Dabbers.

The Craft of Falling Water

ties of Sapphire, Cashiers and Highlands cuts across rivers, creeks, and runs before dropping into the Cullasaja Gorge. Waterfalls abound here, chief among them Dry Falls, which you can walk behind and not get wet (well, almost), and Bridal Veil, which probably qualifies as the first ever drive-through waterfall. The narrow highway, with its hairpin turns and sheer drop offs can be treacherous, but it is arguably one of the single-most beautiful roads in the country. We urge you to enjoy the views and the stops along this route, but with appropriate caution. 〜 The road and the water, like old friends, will part ways for the final leg of the journey to Franklin and on into Cullowhee. When you are done, you will have gained an appreciation for the rich crafts tradition that thrives in this region. 〜 You will also discover that water, in its own way, is the most patient of all crafters. Slowly, over millions of years, it has carved the very faces of these mountains.

Cascades Trail

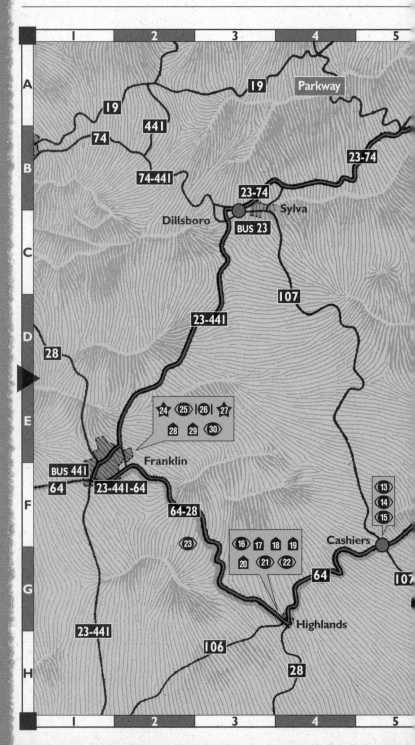

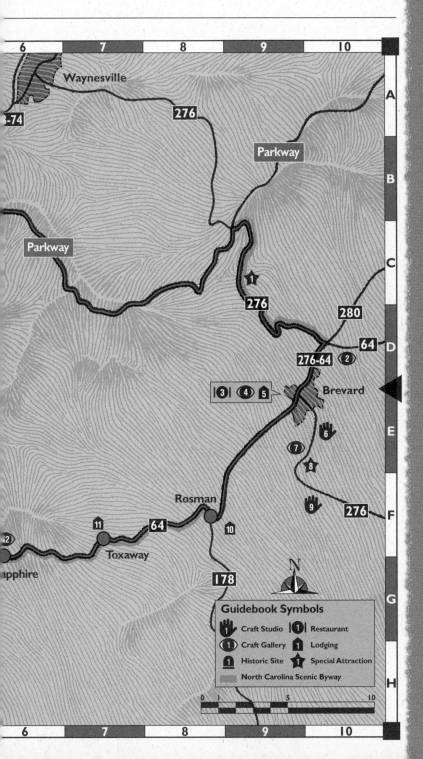

Guidebook Symbols

✋ Craft Studio |🍴| Restaurant

◖1◗ Craft Gallery   🏠 Lodging

🏛 Historic Site   ⭐ Special Attraction

▬ North Carolina Scenic Byway

This lovely two-day excursion measures about 130 miles in length if you return to your starting point. Begin by taking Hwy 276 off the Blue Ridge Parkway south toward your first stop, the Cradle of Forestry.

THE GENUINE ARTICLE
Take one of the trails at the Cradle of Forestry and you'll come across a 1915 Climax steam train once used to haul timber from these mountains. Climb into the cab and discover something even more astonishing: Floyd Rose, the eighty-something custodian who once worked in the logging industry. Wednesday through Saturday he educates folks on the particulars of the train (a geared locomotive) and about how things used to be. The train's impressive, but Floyd is the real find.

PISGAH FOREST

1 **Cradle of Forestry** HWY 276, PISGAH NATIONAL FOREST. This new interpretive center harmonizes nicely with its peaceful setting. Inside, learn the story of Gifford Pinchot, Carl Schenck and the birth of the American forestry movement through short films and engaging exhibits. Two trails lead you back into the woods—and back in time—to the historic dwellings used by the first forestry school students. Small admission charge. Seven days, 9–5 (April 20–Oct 31). "Living History" demonstrations (quilters, weavers, toymakers, and others) Fri–Sun. (704) 877-3130

BREVARD AREA

2 **Southern Expressions** HWY 64, FOUR MILES EAST OF BREVARD. This self-sufficient husband and wife team harvested white and yellow pine on site to build simple, attractive gallery and studio spaces. He's a potter. She's a weaver. A well-selected collection of work, including their own, along with impressive wood pieces from craftspeople local and distant. Tues–Sat, 9–6. (704) 884-6242

3 **Bracken Mountain Bakery** 34 S. BROAD ST., DOWNTOWN. No directions necessary, just follow your nose. Outstanding fresh-baked breads and pastries made from organically grown stone ground flours milled in North Carolina. Darn good coffee, too. Mon–Fri, 8–4; Sat, 9–4. (704) 883-4034

4 **The Frame Up** 4 W. MAIN ST., DOWNTOWN. Don't let the name fool you. The real lure here is the custom craft and the serene environment in which it is presented. Mon–Fri, 10–5; Sat, 10–2. (704) 883-2385

5 **The Inn at Brevard** 410 E. MAIN ST. Built in 1885 for a wealthy widow from Virginia who entertained Lady Astor and other notable personalities. Dining room open to public for lunch, dinner and Sunday brunch. Seats 80. (704) 884-2105

6 **Mountain Forest Studio** THREE MILES SOUTH OF BREVARD ON HWY 276. This 100-year-old farmhouse is almost as charming as Mary Murray, the talented potter who works here. Beautiful flower

The Road Goes On Forever
Side Trips, adventures, and treasure hunts

SLIDING ROCK
Each year, thousands of children and adults slide down sixty feet of pitched granite, propelled by 11,000 gallons of water a minute. It's a quick trip to an unceremonious dunking into a chilly pool. Asked why they do it, most respond with steely resolve, "Because it's there."

gardens out front set the stage for the what you'll find inside. Locals know to stop by on Sundays: that's the day Mary's sister, Susan, tends the gardens (and answers questions). Mon–Sat, 10–5; Sun, 12–5. (704) 885-2149

7 Mud Dabbers' Pottery and Craft FOUR MILES SOUTH OF BREVARD ON HWY 276 AT ROCKBROOK CAMP FOR GIRLS. Work of character by a family of potters. The father, John Dodson, has taught his craft to thousands of summer campers. A wood building dating from the mid-1800's makes a fitting gallery for the works of John, his wife, and their sons and daughters (see sidebar). Mon–Sat, 9–6; Sun, 1–6, year-round. (704) 884-9856

8 Farm Country Store HWY 276, SOUTH OF BREVARD. An old country store whose staples are now cottage crafts, dried flowers, jam, jellies, pickles, relishes and all kinds of other good smelling stuff. Mon–Sat, 8:30–6:30; Sun, 12–5 (mid-Feb–Dec). (704) 883-8798

9 Cedar Mountain Artworks TURN RIGHT OFF HWY 276 JUST PAST SHERWOOD FOREST AND ONTO CEDAR LANE. While pursuing her MFA, Judith Duff took a pottery class "and never got it out of my mind." Lucky for us. Jewel-like glazes and an artist's eye combine to create inspired work. Mon–Sat, 9–5; Sun, 1–5. (704) 884-5258.

ROSMAN

10 Red Lion Inn HWY 178, 13 MILES SOUTH OF BREVARD. Cozy inn by mountain stream. Its reputation for good food—especially fish—extends way beyond county lines. Dinner only. Thurs–Sat, 5:30–8:30. (704) 884-6868.

Spot the farm implements at work in this chair by Brad Smith.

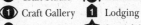

Guidebook Symbols

Craft Studio | Restaurant
Craft Gallery | Lodging
Historic Site | Special Attraction

The artistry of Judith
Duff on display at
Cedar Mountain
Artworks.

TOXAWAY

11 **The Greystone Inn** US 64, 17 MILES WEST OF
BREVARD ON LAKE TOXAWAY. Even the most jaded
world traveler is disarmed by this gentle place
where every conceivable detail has been thought-
fully considered. This Inn's hospitality is reflected
in carefully chosen antiques, an array of activities
from golf to guided hikes, and a menu that offers
fifteen ways to eat trout. Owner Tim Lovelace welcomes passersby to drop in just to look around.
Weekends, Dec, Jan, Feb, and March; open seven
days rest of year. (800) 824-5766

SAPPHIRE

12 **General American Voices** HWY 64 E. The outside may be funky, but inside you will discover
some masterpieces by nationally recognized potters. One in particular has displayed work in the
White House. Mon–Sat, 10–6; Sun, 1–6 (June–
Dec). Fri–Mon, 10–5 (Jan–May). (704) 862-4406

CASHIERS

13 **The Just Plain Ole Fashun Shop** DOGWOOD VIL-
LAGE AT THE CROSSROAD BEHIND THE CHAMBER
OF COMMERCE. Jams, jellies and cottage crafts
from the area. Mon–Sat, 10–5 (April–December).
(704) 743-3164

14 **Main Street Workshop** FOUR MILES FROM CASH-
IERS ON HWY 107. You can always tell a good woodworker by the sign out front. This couple works
well together. Her handmade baskets decorate his
well-crafted furniture. Worth the detour. Seven
days, 10–5. (704) 743-2437

Pottery by
Dennis
Pitter.

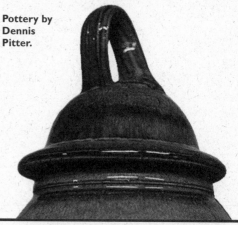

The Road Goes On Forever
Side Trips, adventures,
and treasure hunts

*Moses saw the promised land from Mt. Pisgah.
Inspired by this biblical reference, George Vanderbilt
gave the highest peak on his 100,000 acres the same
name. Sold to the U.S. government after his death,
part of this land became the foundation for the
Pisgah National Forest, now 480,000 acres.*

15 **High Hampton Inn & Country Club** 112 HAMPTON RD. Once the private estate of South Carolina governor and confederate general Wade Hampton. This 1,200 acre family resort epitomizes southern hospitality. Favorite activities include golf, tennis, canoeing, fishing and perambulating the rhododendron. (704) 743-2411

HIGHLANDS

16 **The Custom House** JUST OFF HWY 64 ON CAROLINA WAY. A complimentary blend of American domestic crafts from all over (see the map in the back of the store) and restored antique southern Piedmont furniture. Commissioned reproductions, too. Mon–Sat, 10–5. (704) 526-2665

17 **The Phelps House Inn and Restaurant** END OF MAIN. A notable repeat destination. For people who prefer homey comfort but who like linens and fine china at dinner time. (704) 526-2590

Raku mask by Brad Dodson.

18 **The Old Edwards Inn** 4TH AND MAIN ST. Built in 1878 and rescued in 1981 by Rip and Pat Benton. Most of the 19 country elegant rooms have balconies and private baths with big tubs. Central House Restaurant serves guests and public some noteworthy seafood entrees. (704) 526-5036

19 **Highlands Inn** ACROSS FROM THE OLD EDWARD. Also owned by the Bentons. Constructed 1880, redone 1989. A tad higher fee than Old Edward. Central House serves guests of both inns lunch and dinner. (704) 526-5036

20 **The Old Creek Lodge** 165 NC 106/DILLARD RD. Hidden among evergreens in the middle of Highlands. Fifteen cottages and lodge offer up all the modern conveniences. Informal gardens. (704) 526-2273

A collection of patchwork pins by Helen Coman.

21 **Southern Hands** #1 WRIGHT SQUARE, MAIN ST. Cascading displays of furnishings and high quality regional crafts. Try, but you won't see everything the first time around. Mon–Sat, 10–5; Sun 11–5. (704) 526-4807

22 **Masterworks of Highlands** WRIGHT SQUARE, MAIN ST. Pottery, jewelry, woodwork and other crafts with a contemporary slant. Daily, 10–6. (704) 526-2633.

HIGHLANDS TO FRANKLIN

23 **Muggins Weavery** HWY 64, HALFWAY BETWEEN HIGHLANDS AND FRANKLIN. Looms crowd the floor of this studio and gallery; spools of colorful yarn line the walls. Be very careful turning into

Guidebook Symbols

🖐️❶ Craft Studio	🍴❶ Restaurant
❶ Craft Gallery	🛏️❶ Lodging
❶ Historic Site	⭐❶ Special Attraction

gravel parking area; Muggins sits at a blind curve. Mon–Sat, 10–4, closed Tues. (704) 369-8564

FRANKLIN

24 Franklin Gem and Mineral Museum IN THE OLD JAIL ON COURT HOUSE SQUARE. A safe way to display gems and a jewel of a way to restore an historic building. Mon–Sat, 10–4; Sun, 1–4 (May–Oct). (704) 369-7831

25 Michael Rogers Gallery 218 PALMER ST., AT INTERSECTION OF HWY 441 BUSINESS. Mountain views in watercolor. Mon–Fri, 9–5:30; Sat 9–3. (704) 524-6709

26 Frog and Owl Kitchen 12 E. MAIN ST. Ed Broyles and Jerri Fifer Broyles describe what they offer in this congenial, high ceilinged space as "European food with mountain flair." Literally tranlsated, that means chicken taragon with cheese grits, gingered beef tips with barley, squash bisque and other wondrous intercontinental inspirations. This mountain bistro also offers music on the weekends, typically jazz and folk. Year-round. Mon–Sat, 11am–9pm (704) 349-4112

27 The Tartan Museum 33 E. MAIN ST., FRANKLIN. Acknowledged as a "cultural treasure" by The Year of the Mountains Commission. Here you can identify the particular tartan plaid of a Scottish relative. Exhibits within from 1700 forward, illustrating Celtic heritage. Two handweavers create plaided fabric. Tues–Sat, 10–5; Sun, 1–5 (May–October). Rest of year, Wed–Sat, 10–5. (704) 524-7472

28 The Franklin Terrace A BED AND BREAKFAST ON HIGHWAY 28 TWO BLOCKS FROM MAIN ST. IN FRANKLIN. Originally built as a school in 1887, now known for its sweeping porches and guest rooms romanced with period antiques. Open every day (April 1–Nov. 15). (704) 524-7907

29 Snow Hill Inn 531 SNOW HILL ROAD, FRANKLIN. From Franklin, take 441 to Sanderstown Road, turn right at intersection with SR 228 and drive two and a half miles making a right on Cowee Creek Road, then left fork to Snow Hill Road. Nine rooms, gourmet breakfasts, 14 foot ceilings, and antiques, all in a renovated 1914 school house with 360 degree views. (704) 369-2100

30 Maco Crafts, Inc. TWO MILES SOUTH OF FRANKLIN ON HWY 441 TOWARD ATLANTA. Authentic mountain crafts on three levels. Descend the basement stairs to a quilter's heaven. Overwhelming choice of fabrics and supplies in floor

Hangin' out with Brad Dodson's mountain gnomes.

The Road Goes On Forever
Side Trips, adventures, and treasure hunts

SP☼T IT!
It's somewhere on this loop. Can you find it?

to ceiling displays. Mon–Sat, 10–5 (Nov–May); Mon–Sat, 9–5:30; Sun, 1–5:30 (June–Oct). (704) 524-7878

From Franklin return to the Blue Ridge Parkway via US 23 N and 74 E. On the way, you'll pass the towns of Dillsboro and Sylva, which are described in the Shadow of the Smokies section of this guidebook.

Robert Stephan's glass at Riverwood Menagerie.

A LEGAL DISTILLERY
Bootleg whiskey was once far more commonplace in this region than the legal kind. But there were some who insisted on abiding by the law. "Babe" Cooper operated a federal distillery in a three-story building on the Greenville Highway (US 276) beginning in 1856. The distillery, replete with water wheel and grindstone, remained in business until prohibition. It still stands, today serving as a studio gallery for Mud Dabbers Pottery and offices for Rockbrook Camp.

Forest Heritage Scenic Byway
Waterfall Byway

The Forest Heritage Scenic Byway initiates the Cascades Trail. It's an eventful sixteen miles. The winding descent through the lush Pisgah National Forest leads you to the Cradle of Forestry (see listing), Fish Hatchery, Sliding Rock (bring your swim suit), and Looking Glass Falls.

Pick up the Waterfall Byway near Rosman after traveling a brief distance down US 64. This route is well-named. There are 200 waterfalls surrounding this route, some right along the road. Before reaching the falls though, you will pass through Cashiers and Highlands, resort communities with a hundred year tradition of cooling off parched low country visitors.

Dropping down into the Cullasaja Gorge from Highlands, you will be treated to three waterfalls in succession: Bridal Veil, Dry Falls, and Cullasaja Falls, which drops over 300 feet in just half a mile. The road unknots itself just in time to enter Franklin, a nice place to pause and reflect on a most exhilarating ride.

Guidebook Symbols

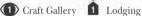

Craft Studio | Restaurant
Craft Gallery | Lodging
Historic Site | Special Attraction

Haywood Community College

HERITAGE

Nurturing Excellence

The allure of production crafts program at Haywood Community College is summed up in the tired, but proud smiles so often found on the faces of its students. "They are doing," says Gary Clontz, clay instructor and department chairperson, "what they love." Approximately 60 students are enrolled in the seemingly all-consuming, seven quarter program. At the end of that period, the instructors hope they've helped the students craft something of lasting value: a lifelong profession.

"We provide a service to craftspeople that no one else is offering," says Clontz, who has been with the school since 1974. "We try to balance the teaching of technical crafts skills with business skills — like how to access the market and start a small business."

But does attention to such practical matters as bookkeeping and marketing interfere with the artistic side of the student's education? The annual Graduating Students Exhibition held every April at the Folk Art Center provides a ready answer.

"It's always one of our most popular shows," says Catherine Duncan, curator of the Southern Highland Craft Guild. "The work is consistently innovative and

Student firing pots.

competes with the highest caliber of craft being produced anywhere in the country."

That the work remains outstanding from year to year is testament to the

The weaving studio.

school's instructors. In addition to Clontz, the faculty includes Arch Gregory, instructor in jewelry; Robert Gibson, design and photography; Catharine Muerdter, fiber; and Wayne Raab, wood.

Graduates become walking testimonials when asked about the two years spent with these patient teachers. "The whole time you're there, the instructors treat you as if you're a professional craftsperson," says Sarah Wells Roland, a 1989 graduate. "We were so well taken care of it was almost frightening to leave."

But leave they do, and often to a promising future. "When I arrived at Haywood, I'd never touched clay," remembers Roland. "By the time I graduated, I was wholesaling and marketing my work."

"Walking Dresser"
by Juanita Huryn.

PHOTO: SARA HATTON
ALL OTHER PHOTOS: BARRET RUDICH

Shadow of the Smokies

In the 1880s, the first trains arrived in the mountains, and with them visitors from all over the world. Re sorts sprang up within a carriage ride of each railway stop. Fanciful places like the Eagle's Nest. White Sulphur Springs. The Balsam Manor Inn. The Randolph House. And the Yankee Hipps Hotel. △ They arrived in cars, pulled by locomotives, coming from cities where industry was worshipped, to find a world still unaffected by combustion engines, machinery, and electricity. A world where mass production was a matter of doing one thing—well. Where even the most common of objects arrived without peer—each carrying the personality of its maker. The curve of a chairback. The pattern of a basket. The weave of a blanket. △ These visitors to the mountains found something they'd lost in their mad dash toward progress and the dazzle of the future. And they soon found themselves champions of its preservation. △ This tour begins where the railroad, coming up from Georgia, made its first stop after cresting the mountains, at the tiny station in

Passions in repose at Collene Karcher's marble studio near Sylva

Objects Without Peer

Balsam. A short distance further on is the town of Waynesville, still welcoming visitors with the same home-spun charm and good will as it did a century ago. Cross Soco Gap and you will alight in a place whose craft heritage predates our country. The spirit of the American Indian remains unbowed in the objects you will find here. Ceremonial masks and pottery. Finely detailed wood sculpture. Baskets of river cane, split white oak, and honeysuckle vine. Following the train track from Bryson City, you will come to a place that feels like a homecoming. In Dillsboro, visitors abandon their cars for the pleasures of ambling along tidy streets. Its avenues are filled with places where craft isn't just sold, but is joyously conjured up before your very eyes. And here, if you're so inclined, you can still ride the rails behind a steam locomotive. Stay in the Shadow of the Smokies, and you eventually land at a point where so many others have come before you. It's a place where a handmade object can, in its own simple way, balance the progress of an entire century.

Shadow of the Smokies

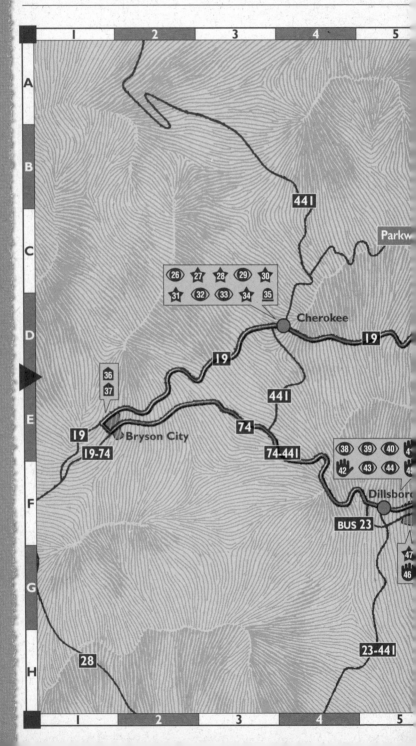

441

Parkw

26 27 28 29 30
31 32 33 34 35

Cherokee

19

19

36
37

441

19

19-74

⏵ Bryson City

74

74-441

38 39 40 4
42 43 44 4

Dillsbor

BUS 23

47
46

28

23-441

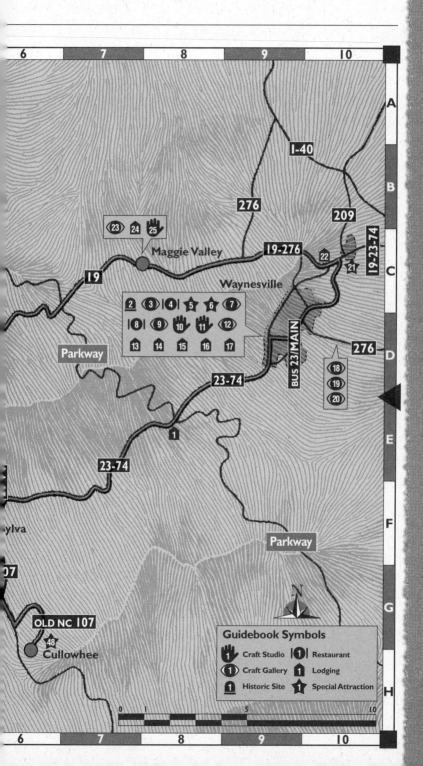

Guidebook Symbols

- Craft Studio
- Craft Gallery
- Historic Site
- Restaurant
- Lodging
- Special Attraction

This loop is the most compact in distance yet is saturated with fascinations. Allow two or three days, and plan on driving a hundred miles. Enter at the Parkway's intersection with US 23/74, west of Waynesville.

The timeless beauty of the Balsam Manor Inn.

1 Balsam Manor Inn MAKE RIGHT ON US 23/74 EXITING PARKWAY. ONE HALF MILE DOWN, WATCH FOR SIGN: "BALSAM INN NEXT LEFT." Opened in 1908 to serve the highest railway depot east of the Rockies, this three-story inn offers an abundance of porches, rockers and wonderful food. It boasts few modern conveniences—like room phones and TV—and that's just fine. Also home to Autumn Showcase, a dandy exhibition of local art, craft and music. Reservations advised for accommodations and meals. Year-round. (704) 456-9498

Follow 19/23 northeast to Waynesville.

DOWNTOWN WAYNESVILLE

2 N.C. Handicraft Museum IN THE SHELTON HOUSE, CORNER OF 276 (PIGEON ST.) AND SHELTON ST. Built in 1875, this museum is home to work exhibited at the N.C. State Fair. Standouts include Indian artifacts, handwoven coverlets and quilts, and the work of master potters. Wed–Sat, 10:30–4. (704) 452-1551

3 Haywood Handcraft Co-op 121 S. MAIN ST. A hard-to-miss building at the head of Main St. houses affordable cottage crafts. Mon–Sat, 10–5. (704) 452-7662

4 Lomo Grill CHURCH ST. Candy roasters, garden grown herbs, farmer's market vegetables and local Rainbow Trout complement a continental menu. This beautifully restored space comes with tin ceiling and exposed brick walls. Mon–Sat, 11:30–3, 5:30–10. (704) 452-5222

5 Blue Owl 115 CHURCH ST. Old postcard photographs are the basis for the handcolored prints you'll find here. Historic hotels, public buildings, and scenic vistas evoke childhood memories of these mountains. Mon–Sat 10–5. (704) 456-5050

6 T. Pennington Art Gallery 106 N. MAIN ST. Sights in Waynesville and Asheville are subjects of this artist's colored pencil creations. Originals and signed and numbered prints available in custom frames. Mon–Sat, 10–5. (704) 452-9284

7 Earthworks 110 N. MAIN ST. Environmentally-focused, with Indian handcrafts that inspire a feeling of harmony. Cherokee crafts receive emphasis, along with other American tribes. Mon–Sat, 10–5. (704) 452-9500

The Road Goes On Forever
Side Trips, adventures, and treasure hunts

SPOT IT!
It's somewhere on this loop. Can you find it?

8 Whitman's Bakery 113 N. MAIN ST. The true seat of power in Waynesville isn't in city hall. It's at one of the tables in this popular local establishment. Expansive lunch menu and comfortable booths encourage lingering. It's impossible to get in or out without passing two huge glass cases filled with goodies. Shame on them. Bakery, 6am–5:30pm; sandwich counter, 11am–3pm. (704) 456-8271

9 Balsam Gallery 119 N. MAIN ST. You might call the proprietor of this gallery a crafter of space. With surprises and discoveries at every turn, you'll find yourself thinking, "What's next?" and never be disappointed. Mon–Sat, 10–5. (704) 452-2524

10 Whitewoven Handweaving Studio and Gallery 201 MAIN ST. Climb a flight of steps and run right into the biggest loom you've ever seen. Rugs from this loom rarely get walked upon. Folks prefer to hang them in places usually reserved for art. Tues–Fri, 11–5. (704) 452-4864

11 Burr Studio and Gallery 261 N. WALL ST. This tiny, backstreet space welcomes visitors with open arms. The arms—and the talent—belong to Dane and MaryEtta Burr, sculptor and potter, respectively. Established craftspeople still taking risks. Mon–Sat, 10–5; Sun, 12–5. (704) 456-7400

12 The Glass Giraffe 110 DEPOT ST. Look for the art deco glass brick on the facade. It's a tip-off to what's inside. Glass as jewelry, as decorative frames, as sun-catchers and more. Classes also offered. Mon–Fri, 10–6; Sat, 11–6. (704) 456-6665

WAYNESVILLE INNS AND B & B'S

13 Grandview Lodge 809 VALLEY VIEW CIRCLE ROAD, OFF ALLEN'S CIRCLE ROAD. A country inn where Linda Arnold's food—from carrot soup to rhubarb pie—steals the show. Call ahead for dinner reservations. (704) 456-5212 or (800) 255-7826

14 Herren House 200 EAST ST. North Carolina quilts grace every bed in this spacious house. Call ahead for dinner reservations. (704) 452-7837

15 Belle Meade Inn 804 BALSAM RD. A craftsman-style house dating from 1908 with chestnut woodwork and a large stone fireplace to take the chill off cool mountain evenings. (704) 456-3234

16 The Old Stone Inn (formerly Heath Lodge) 900 DOLAN RD. Families have come back to the same room, the same week of the year, for decades. Some things get better with time. Rustic accommodations and heaven-sent food. Call for dinner reservations. (704) 456-3333

COLORS FROM THE EARTH.

Basket weavers use natural dyes for staining individual strips of river cane, honeysuckle vine and split oak. These dye colors come from these sources:

Orange
Butternut

Brown
Walnut

Dark Brown
Bloodroot

Burnt Orange-Dk. Red
Wild Coreopsis

Yellow
Broom sedge grass

Chartreuse
Smartweed/Cocklebur

Red
Poke Berries

Tan
Acorns

Dark Yellow/Tan
Apple Bark

TAKE A PEAK.
Within the borders of Haywood County, there are 19 peaks of over 6,000 feet.

Guidebook Symbols

Craft Studio   Restaurant

Craft Gallery   Lodging

Historic Site   Special Attraction

Top: Potter Benjamin
Burns applies a glaze.

Above: One of
Benjamin's lobster
plates.

17 **Ten Oaks** 803½ LOVE LANE, OFF DELLWOOD RD. Turn-of-the-century colonial revival-style house was once the center of Waynesville society. No less impressive today. (704) 452-4373

OF NOTE NEAR WAYNESVILLE

18 **Wood'n'Craft Shop** FOUR MILES SOUTH OF WAYNESVILLE ON 276. Cabin features a variety of craft, and especially the inspired wood sculpture of shop owner Ron Mayhew. This is work in search of a museum. Mon–Sat, 10–5. (704) 235-8607

19 **Signatures in Fine Crafts** 339 PISGAH DR. (turn left on Hwy 110 two miles beyond Ron Mayhew's and drive another two miles). Carroll Van Zee welcomes you with decorative, functional pottery and conversation. Tues–Sat, 10–5. (704) 648-2900

20 **Cruso Crafts Co-op** THIRTEEN MILES SOUTH OF WAYNESVILLE ON 276. Old rock school house is fitting showcase for cottage crafts made by members of a local homemakers club. Annual quilt show in August features quilts dating from late 1800s. 10–4, Mon–Sat (June–Oct). (704) 235-8497

21 **Haywood Community College** FIVE MILES EAST OF WAYNESVILLE ON US 19/23. Exit at Jones Cove Road and, once on campus, drive to top of hill, turn right at stop sign and look for Production Crafts Building on right. This school, known throughout the region for its distinguished craft program, invites passers by to stop and enjoy a view into working studios. Student craft work, always of high caliber, is often on display. (704) 627-4670

22 **The Lambuth Inn** AT JUNALUSKA, ON US 19 TO-WARD MAGGIE VALLEY. An architecturally enchanting inn above the lake, listed on the National Register. Private reservations are welcome most of the year. Across the street from the Harrell Center Heritage Museum, displaying historic crafts. Seasonal rates. Dining. (704) 452-2887

IN MAGGIE VALLEY

23 **The Different Drummer** US 19. Wheel-thrown functional porcelain and stoneware featuring scribbled glazes in blue and green. Terance Painter's fine work is used at the Cataloochee Ranch. Year-round, Mon–Sat, 9–5. (704) 926-3850

24 **Cataloochee Ranch** FIE TOP RD. OFF US 19. A 1,000-acre guest ranch that's really it's own little mountain-top world. Family-style meals featuring Southern Appalachian specials served in a rustic lodge. How do people feel about this special place? Just read the guest book. Seven days. Breakfast,

---

The Road Goes On Forever

Side Trips, adventures, and treasure hunts

BORROWED TECHNOLOGY
The Cherokee people have thrown pots for over 4,000 years (but they did "pick up" the idea from the Catawbas about the time of the Bronze Age in Egypt).

8–9; lunch, 12:30; dinner, 6 and 7:30 (April–Oct). Reservations recommended. (704) 926-1401

Pitter The Potter ONE MILE SOUTH OF GHOST TOWN ON US 19. Drive slowly and look quickly. (It's on your right as you leave Maggie Valley.) There are three accomplished potters here, Dennis Pitter, his wife, Linda, and Benjamin Burns. All share a passion for craft and conversation. You can learn a lot. Year-round, daily. (704) 926-6258

CHEROKEE

Big Meat House of Pottery US 19, ONE MILE NORTH OF CHEROKEE. The Big Meat family have been potters for generations. In addition to low-fired coil pottery that turns into wedding vases and medicine bowls, you'll also see high quality masks, pipes, knives, basketry, and beaded jewelry. Mon–Sat, 9–5 (May–Oct). (704) 497-9544

Talking Leaves Book Store 441 AND US 19. Small exhibit of fine Cherokee crafts along with wide selection of Cherokee and other Native American books. 10–5, (May–Oct). (704) 497-6044

Museum of the Cherokee Indians US 441 ON LEFT AT LARGE CHEROKEE STATUE. The complete history of the Cherokees from the Ice Age to the present; treaties, language, artifacts, and stories. Mon–Sat, 9–8; Sun, 9–5 (mid-June to August). Daily, 9–5 (Sept–mid-June). $4 adults/$2 children. (704) 497-3481

Qualla Arts & Crafts Gallery US 441 BESIDE MUSEUM. They call themselves "the most outstanding Indian-owned and operated cooperative in America." They're right. Look for river cane, split oak, and honeysuckle vine baskets of peerless quality, along with ceremonial masks, low-fire pottery and wood carvings. Daily, 9–4:30. (704) 497-3103

Oconaluftee Indian Village US 441. Step back in time and see Cherokee Indian life as it was, not how it's been portrayed in movies and television. The earliest forms of American craft—pottery, basket making, wood carving, and weaving—are demonstrated and sustained here. 9–5:30 (May–Oct). $9 adults/$5 children. (704) 497-2111

The exquisite handwork of the Cherokee at the Qualla Co-op Store.

Unto These Hills Outdoor Drama US 441. Mid-June through August, nightly except Sunday. Tickets reserved in advance or purchased at box office. (704) 497-2111

Medicine Man Crafts US 441 N. Owner Tom Underwood's devotion to craft and his encouragement of local craftspeople is much in evidence.

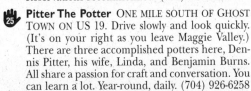

Guidebook Symbols

Craft Studio   Restaurant

Craft Gallery   Lodging

Historic Site   Special Attraction

Rick Urban at the wheel.

Heat is what makes it ceramic. Until then, it's just dirt.

Brant Barnes, potter, on the clay firing process.

Hammered bowl and spoon at Riverwood Pewter Shop.

Pay notice to the wood sculptures and ask about their makers. Year-round, 9–5. (704) 497-2202

(33) **Trail of Tears Gallery** ACQUONI ROAD. Authentic Cherokee crafts under the stewardship of someone who knows and loves every item in this gallery. Seven days, 10–10 (March–Nov); 10–5 (Nov–Dec); closed Jan–Feb. (704) 497-3243

(34) **Mountain Farm Museum** GREAT SMOKY MOUNTAINS NATIONAL PARK. US 441 AT PARK ENTRANCE. Discover the ways and wiles of early farm life. Daily, 9am–10pm (March–Nov 15). Thurs–Sun, 10:30–5 (Mid-Nov–Feb). (704) 497-1900

(35) **Mingus Mill** GREAT SMOKY MOUNTAINS NATIONAL PARK. US 441 AT PARK ENTRANCE. Experience the thud, clank and spin of grinding corn. Daily, 9–5 (April–October). (704) 497-1900

BRYSON CITY

(36) **Fryemont Inn and Restaurant** JUST UP FROM MAIN ST. On the National Register of Historic Places. Boasts an enticing menu featuring trout served four ways, baked Virginia ham and other savories. Daily, April–October. (704) 488-2159

(37) **Randolph House Country Inn** NEXT TO FRYEMONT INN. Also on the register, this intimate inn celebrated its centennial in 1995. Good things last. Daily, April–October (704) 488-3472

DILLSBORO

(38) **Carlon's** 134 HAYWOOD RD., NEXT TO JARRETT HOUSE. Reasonably-priced collection of practical crafts, including pottery, quilts, and wood pieces. 10:30–5:30 (April–December). (704) 369-6041

(39) **Dogwood Crafters** WEBSTER ST., ONE BLOCK SOUTH OF JARRETT HOUSE. Looks like a rustic log cabin but is actually one of the most extensive collections of cottage craft anywhere. See if you can find the back. Daily, 9:30–9. (704) 586-2248

(40) **The Mountain Pottery** FRONT ST. Rick Urban, escapee from Madison Avenue, has successfully eluded capture for over 10 years by posing as a contented potter. Watch this former ad guy at his wheel or treat yourself to the work of the 50 other potters whose work is displayed in this cheerful, sun-filled space. Seven days, 10–5. (704) 586-9183

(41) **Riverwood Menagerie** ACROSS RIVER FROM DILLSBORO. Be surrounded by stained glass in a multitude of shapes and colors. Get caught up watching the creation of a new work and you won't want to leave. Mon–Sat, 10–5. (704) 586-9083

The Road Goes On Forever

Side Trips, adventures, and treasure hunts

ALL ABOARD!
This steam train, built in Philadelphia in 1942, now takes passengers on excursions between Dillsboro and Bryson City. For the next departure, call the Smoky Mountain Railway. (704) 586-8811

Riverwood Pottery RIVERWOOD SHOPS. Affable potter Brant Barnes loves to cook. Consequently, most everything he offers works in the kitchen. His wife, Karen, is the creator of the wall sconces and vases. Intriguing borders, dynamic colors, and good vibrations abound. 10–5. (704) 586-3601

Nature's Trail Gallery RIVERWOOD SHOPS. Decorative gourds and masks based on traditional Native American motifs in an artful setting. Mon–Sat, 10–5 (April–December); Thurs–Sat, 10–5 (Jan–March). (704) 524-7182.

Oaks Gallery RIVERWOOD SHOPS. The only thing that overshadows the work in this intimate gallery is the 300-year-old oak towering over it. Especially fine bowls, kitchenware and jewelry sold by people who care. Mon–Sat, 10–5 (April–Dec); Thurs–Sat, 10–5 (Jan–March). (704) 586-6542

Riverwood Pewter Shop RIVERWOOD SHOPS. A fascinating process wherein thin pewter sheets are pounded into molds to make tea pots and sets, napkin holders, and Jefferson cups. The product is simple elegance. Mon–Sat, 10–5 (April–Dec); Thurs–Sat, 10–5 (Jan–March). (704) 586-6996

SYLVA

Karcher Stone Carving Studio 40 N. BETA RD. EXIT US 74 AT SCOTTS CREEK CHURCH ROAD. Turn left onto Old Asheville Hwy and almost immediately right on N. Beta Rd. What's a sculptor, classically trained in Rhode Island and Italy, doing in a 100-year-old chestnut barn near Sylva? Don't ask. Just marvel at the figurative pieces she wrests from 1600 pound blocks of Alabama marble. Other startling works in bronze, alabaster, blackstone and wood. Mon–Sat, 10–5. (704) 586-4813.

An ecstacy of form. Stone carving by Collene Karcher.

City Lights Bookstore and Cafe 3 E. JACKSON ST. Sip coffee from hand-crafted mugs, browse shelves laden with mind-boggling words, and study over imaginative items on loan (or for sale) from regional artisans. Bookstore: Mon–Sat, 9–8. Cafe: Mon–Wed, 9–8; Thurs–Sat, 9–10. (June–October). Winter hours vary. (704) 586-9499.

CULLOWHEE

Mountain Heritage Center GROUND FLOOR OF ROBINSON ADMIN. BUILDING, WCU. Exhibits, and oftentimes demonstrations, which illustrate the importance of craft-making in Southern Appalachian history. Mon–Fri, 8–5; Sun, 2–5. (704) 227-7129.

Stained glass window at Riverwood Menagerie by Ivor Pace.

HERITAGE

John C. Campbell Folk School

The Art of Sharing

John C. Campbell Folk School is maybe the only school you'll ever find where you can take a course entitled "Hand-planed bamboo fly rod," "Hammering a tune on the hammered dulci-

mer," "Bending jigs for fun and profit," "Gnomes," or "Making a tear-drop fiddle."

It's a place where you can butt things, fuse things, throw things, hook things, join things, and splatter things, then step back from it and clog til the cows come home. And it is as it should be, on this small piece of earth near Brasstown where, in a true collaboration, the community founded a school based on ideas brought forward by John and Olive Dame Campbell.

The Campbells had come to the mountains of the South in 1908, as hu-manitarians, to study the re-gion and its people. As John interviewed farmers about their practices, Olive collected ancient ballads and a variety of contempo-rary handcrafts.

Olive Dame Campbell & Marguerite Butler on their return from Europe.

After John died in 1919, Olive and her friend Marguerite Butler traveled to Europe to look at Danish "schools for life." They returned to the U.S. determined to

Keith House – the community room is on the left.

offer the same kind of opportunity in Appalachia. With land donated by a local family and the sincere support of nearby mountain people, an institution was born in 1925.

"Higher learning" at Campbell Folk School, from its beginnings, has been seated in the soul. As Director Jan Davidson puts it, the school "seeks to bring people toward two kinds of development: inner growth as creative thoughtful individuals, and social development as tolerant, caring members of a community."

Come to Campbell of a summer evening, and you will most likely find families and friends knotted together, speaking excitedly in the strange dialects of craft: kiln temperatures, woofs and warps, slumps and fuses, mortices and tenons, dove-tailing and hand-gouging. After a week or two, or longer, these students will return home—to the farm, to the city—taking with them something of what John and Olive originally intended. Something about themselves, tucked away, in a suitcase or knapsack, in the shape of a quite wonderful object of their own hand.

The Lake Country

In the first half of this century, a series of dams were constructed on the Hiawasee, Nantahala and Little Tennessee rivers. In addition to creating electricity, the dams transformed what were once dry hollows and coves into a series of many-fingered lakes that give this trail its name. ✦ The lakes brought with them both opportunity and heartache. Homes, churches and farms were lost to the rising waters. But one thing could not be washed away: the strong sense of community so firmly rooted here in the small towns and villages that populate this region. ✦ The crafts of this trail are the crafts of community. Along the way you will find handiwork in finely stitched lace and forged iron, but you will also find it in homespun tales and well-made music and intricately woven dances. ✦ That spirit is joyously embodied at the John C. Campbell Folk School in Brasstown. For eight decades, Saturday night dances have brought to-

"I Sing Behind the Plow.' the symbol of the John C. Campbell Folk School, wrought in copper by the school's first blacksmith, Oscar Cantrell.

The Craft of Community

gether students and local citizens on the old oak dance floor of the school community room. Here, to the sounds of guitar, banjo and fiddle, enduring friendships begin with the simple call to "change partners."  Fellowship, in a slightly less exhuberant form, is also found every day in the literally hundreds of classes the schools offers. Depending on your interest, and the amount of time you have to devote, you can learn to spin yarn, cane a chair, throw a pot, forge a knife, weave a basket, or carve a walking stick. In these classrooms, and in the many different studios you will visit along the way, talented potters, wood carvers, weavers and blacksmiths reveal the "craft" of their work. In return, students and visitors offer their interest and enthusiasm. This, then, is the true communion of craft; for in this sharing between one another, we find that we are all both givers and receivers.

The Lake Country

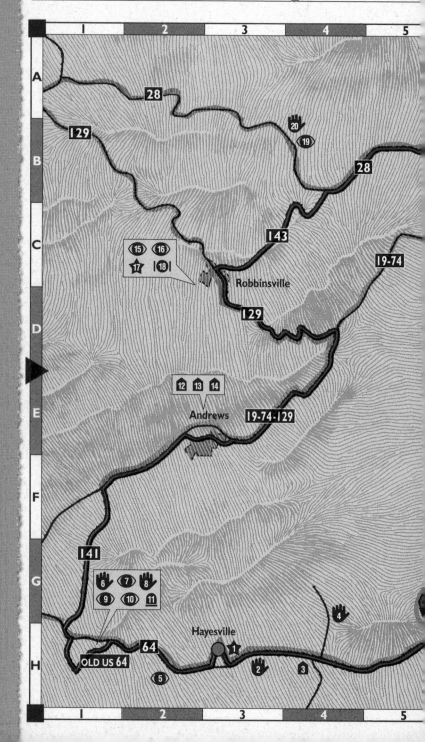

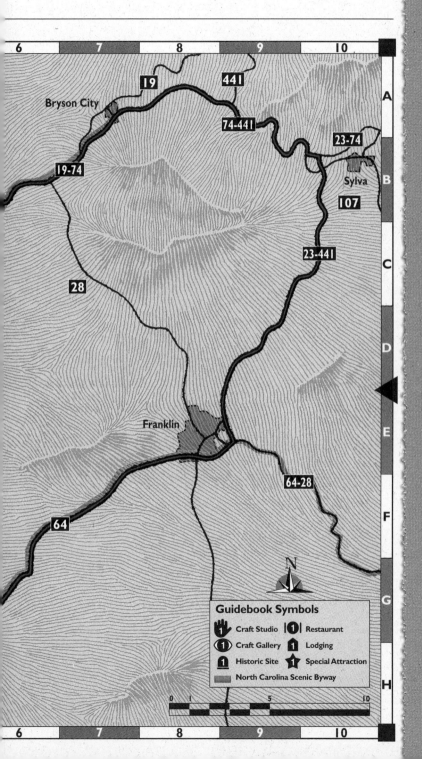

Bryson City

Sylva

Franklin

19

441

74-441

23-74

19-74

107

23-441

28

64-28

64

N

Guidebook Symbols

Craft Studio | Restaurant

Craft Gallery | Lodging

Historic Site | Special Attraction

North Carolina Scenic Byway

0 1   5   10

6   7   8   9   10

A B C D E F G H

You can access this loop by picking it up toward the end of the Cascades Trail. Should you come directly from the Parkway, follow these directions: exit at Balsam, take US 74 to Dillsboro, then 23/441 to Franklin. Total distance, from Franklin through "Lake Country" and back to Parkway amounts to about 165 miles. Total touring time: figure a day and a half at an unrushed, "slow to middlin" pace.

David Goldhagen's glass furnace (above) and one of his color-filled menorahs.

FRANKLIN

An excellent jumping off place for "Lake Country." See Franklin listings in the Cascades tour.

HAYESVILLE AREA

1 **People's Store** HAYESVILLE TOWN SQUARE. Open Monday through Friday provided the proprietor doesn't have something better to do. "Cutworm" offers colas from the old cooler with a hand hanging out of it, as if somebody had got shut up in there. He has doctor's tools and gory tales about limbs cut off with a kitchen knife. Strange things hang out in People's Store, but few of them are for sale. (704) 389-8536

The next three listings are all to be found east of Haysville, off Hwy 64.

2 **Goldhagen Art Glass Studio** TURN RIGHT OFF HWY 64, ONE MILE EAST OF HAYESVILLE, at lone willow tree and sign that says "Hinton Rural Life Center." Drive 2 miles. Watch for blue mailbox on right. Lofted space offers a bird's-eye view of this mesmerizing process. Molten glass is rolled and pulled and stretched into ethereal shapes that appear fluid even after they harden. Mon–Fri, 9–5. (704) 389-8847

3 **Broadax Inn and Restaurant, formerly Elf School** TURN RIGHT ON HWY 175 OFF OF HWY 64 AND WATCH FOR SIGNS. Named for the indelicate companion of local timbermen, this restored 1928 school house features high ceilings and warmly informative hosts. Restaurant, converted from classrooms, also earns a high grade. Year-round. (704) 389-6987.

4 **St. Pierre Wood Pottery** 1 COMPASS MEADOWS. Five miles east of Hayesville, take left off Hwy 64 onto Cold Branch Road (#1330). At four miles, turn right at general store. Studio a quarter of a mile down on left. Robert St. Pierre casts his eye over the various stacks of hardwood in his studio and says "every piece of wood in here has something to offer." Walk a few steps into his gallery

The Road Goes On Forever

Side Trips, adventures, and treasure hunts

There are lots of enjoyable stops in Clay County, but there's only one mandatory one. The stop light in Hayesville is the only such light in the county.

and find out just how much. Bowls, vases, urns, lamps and boxes not turned, but built up, layer upon layer and finely finished. Daily, 9–5. (704) 389-6639

⑤ Walnut Acres Country Store HWY 64, THREE MILES WEST OF THE TRAFFIC LIGHT IN HAYESVILLE. Next door to a gem shop. One room showcase of metalwork, furniture, pottery and other worldly temptations. Tues–Sun, 10–5. (704) 389-4490.

BRASSTOWN AREA

Five miles west of Hayesville's stop light, turn left on Settawig Rd.

⑥ Smith Craft TURN LEFT AT "T" INTERSECTION IN BRASSTOWN. Drive one mile, turn left on first gravel road. Octogenarian Fred Smith knows a thing or two about gouging bowls and trays from native woods. Some fifty years ago he planted the trees he is now harvesting for his celebrated work. For credentials, just call the Smithsonian. Daily, 10–5. (704) 837-2274

Above and opposite: Wood vessels sprung from the imagination of Robert St. Pierre.

From Smith Craft, retrace your steps to Brasstown and to the four "Village Crafters," listed below.

⑦ Round & Smooth Wood Peter Chapman's wood puzzles include a giant snake to wrap around the coffee table. Or your Aunt Gurty's feet. Polished work from polished crafters. Mon–Sat, 9–5. (704) 837-8663

⑧ Persimmon Creek Studios Not just purveyors of craft, practitioners. Terry carves; Kay weaves. But this personable couple can tell you just as much about other people's work as their own. Mon–Sat, 9–5. (704) 837-4132

⑨ Angel Works Heaven-sent collection of natural fiber clothing, linens, everlasting flowers and herbs, and hand-dipped candles. Mon–Sat, 9–5. (704) 837-2222

⑩ Rebekah's Pottery A contemporary potter with a reverence for those who preceded her. Authentic southern folk pottery and work from local masters make a happy marriage. Mon–Sat, 9–5 (April–Dec). Tues–Sat, 11–4 (Jan–Mar). (704) 837-0529

Fred Smith shows off his celebrated work.

⑪ John C. Campbell Folk School BRASSTOWN. Lessons in craft and community are at the heart of this institution founded in 1925. Renowned instructors from throughout the region teach a multitude of disciplines on a charmed 325-acre campus. The work of over 300 craftspeople, including pieces made by the famous Brasstown carv-

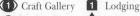

Guidebook Symbols

🖐1 Craft Studio		I●I Restaurant	
①1 Craft Gallery		🛏 Lodging	
🏛1 Historic Site		⭐ Special Attraction	

ers, may be found in the school's craft shop. (See larger description of school in this loop chapter.) Mon–Sat, 9–5; Sun, 1–5. 1-800-FOLK-SCH

From Brasstown turn onto old Hwy 64, then left on new Hwy 64 for a short distance. Turn right on 141 following that highway to its intersection with US 19/74 and on to Andrews.

ANDREWS

12 Walker Inn 39 JUNALUSKA RD, JUST OFF US 19 BUSINESS, EAST OF ANDREWS. This fine old colonial-style inn on the National Register has been welcoming visitors since before the Civil War. Step across the threshold and into a world of bubble-glass window panes, heirlooms, and gatherings around the grand piano. Five guest rooms. Open April–Nov. (704) 321-5019

13 The Cover House 34 WILSON ST. Turn-of-the-century home of Giles and Lilly May Cover. Lilly May was the first woman elected to the North Carolina legislature. Giles convened the nightly gatherings of the menfolk over at Lee Watkin's Feed Store. In addition to a sense of history, guests can relish the fine antiques, clawfoot tubs, and dandy views of the Snowbird Mountains. (704) 321-5302

14 The Hawkesdene House TURN RIGHT OFF US 74 INTO ANDREWS. Right on Cherry St., 3.3 miles to Phillips Creek Rd. Left .5 miles to sign. The English country charm here is authentic. Daphne Sargent hails from Windsor, England. She and her husband Roy welcome guests to this attractive B&B adjoining the Nantahala National Forest. Adding to the fairyland atmosphere are two resident llamas, Hawke and Dene, who will carry your lunch on trail hikes to Hidden Falls and other enchanted spots in the forest. Four guest rooms; two small cottages. (704) 321-6027; (800) 447-9549

Take 19/74 to 129 into Robbinsville.

ROBBINSVILLE

15 Graham Crackers Too ON 129 AT FIRST ROBBINSVILLE INTERSECTION. Spirited gathering of thing-a-ma-bobs, doo-hickies, and whats-its proudly presented by a group of local who-dunits. Tues–Sat, 9–5; Sun, 1–6. (704) 479-2224

16 The Original Graham Crackers TURN LEFT OFF OF 129 INTO DOWNTOWN. LEFT AGAIN ON MAIN. Storefront situated on the downhill side of a local church. Cottage crafts and collectibles in all denominations. Mon–Sat, 10–5. (704) 479-3937.

Top: A collaborative effort by a group of Campbell Folk School blacksmith instructors.

Middle: A forge at the ready.

Bottom: A "chance" of pigs, the proud offspring of one of the Brasstown carvers.

The Road Goes On Forever

Side Trips, adventures, and treasure hunts

HAVE YOU SEEN A CHUNKY GAL?
Legend has it that a young Cherokee maiden from this region ran off with a brave from another tribe. Her envious friends, in a pique of envy, nicknamed her Chunky Gal. And an undulating line of Clay County mountains acquired the name as well.

17 **Graham County Chamber of Commerce** MAIN
STREET. Well-presented crafts displays featuring
work of New Horizons Guild members. Mon–Fri,
9–5. (704) 479-3790.

18 **Phillips Restaurant** MAIN STREET. According to
Roma, who often picks up the phone, "Everybody
eats here." It's no wonder. Country ham, pork
chops, half-fried chicken, perch, trout, catfish, and
the best burgers in town. Also breakfast and dinner buffets. Seven days, 6am–8pm. (704) 479-3332

19 **Johnny Reb Crafts** HWY 143 TO HWY 28, TURN
LEFT TOWARD FONTANA, FIVE MILES. Well-settled
log cabin will surprise you with what it holds. First-
rate pottery, wood carving and other original finds.
Daily, 9–9 (May–Oct). (704) 479-8519

20 **Yellow Branch Pottery** TURN RIGHT TWO MILES
PAST JOHNNY REB'S ONTO YELLOW BRANCH ROAD
(SR 1267). ONE HALF MILE ON RIGHT. You can
sample Karen's own "Yellow Branch" cheeses from
one of her turned dishes. Or you can simply enjoy
the beauty of her unique glazes in the joyous se-
renity of a mountain cove. Mon, Wed–Sat, 2–5
(April–Oct). (704) 479-6710

*May the warp be the
white light of morning,
May the weft be the
red light of evening,
May the fringes be the
falling rain,
May the border be the
standing rainbow,
Thus weave for us a
garment of brightness.*

Song of the Sky Loom
(North American
Indian)

*Return to Parkway (Balsam entrance) driving US 28 to US 19 N, then
to US 74 at Sylva.*

Waterfalls
Nantahala
Indian Lakes

Parts of three Scenic Byways beckon travelers motoring this trail. On the
Waterfalls Byway, west of Franklin, the mountains relax their grip long enough
to allow the emergence of fields and pastures in quilt-like sections.

A few miles after picking up the Nantahala Byway at Marble, the mountains
crowd up again to create one of the most remote—and breathtaking—areas
in the southern Appalachian region.

While not on the loop itself, the section of the Nantahala Byway between
Topton and Almond is highly recommended. This 20-mile journey takes
you through the Nantahala Gorge where the Nantahala River bounces, jolts
and flabbergasts people of all ages in some of the region's liveliest whitewater.

The Lakes Trail also picks up two sections of the Indian Lakes Scenic Byway,
between Robbinsville and Topton on US 129, and between Stecoah and Almond on NC 28, before rejoining the Nantahala Byway. You may wish to
extend the trail by following the entire length of the Indian Lakes Scenic
Byway. Significant stops along the way include the resort community of
Fontana and Fontana Dam, the highest dam in the Eastern United States.

SPOT IT!
It's somewhere
on this loop.
Can you find it?

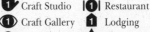

Guidebook Symbols
Craft Studio | Restaurant
Craft Gallery | Lodging
Historic Site | Special Attraction

Index

Index

Index

T

Credits & Thanks

Authors
Jay Fields and Brad Campbell

Design, Photography
Mark Wilson
   Berdahl Smith Wilson Advertising,
   Asheville, NC

Project Coordinator
(Research, Authentication, Travel
Arrangements, Group Conscience)
Robin Daniel

Listing Copy
Jay Fields, Brad Campbell and
Robin Daniel

Design Associate
Helen Robinson
   Berdahl Smith Wilson Advertising

Design Assistants
Lowell Allen
Kristi Pfeffer

Map Design
Eric Stevens

Map Research
Alan Lang and Tom House
   NC Division of
   Community Assistance

Copy Editor
Cathy Mitchell
   Mass Communication Department,
   UNC-Asheville

Index
Lisa Thickitt

Birch Bark
Eric Baden

Administrative Assistant, Superwoman
Sassi McClellan
   HandMade in America

Production Management
Jennifer Clary,
Hickory Printing Group

Printing
Hickory Printing Group
Printed on Springhill Incentive
   Supplied by Dillard Paper
   (Thanks to Ellyn Wells)

Typography
Headlines: Oregonian
   (This delightful face is an original
   design, just for this guidebook, by
   Eric Stevens. Thanks, Eric.)
Subheads: Gill Sans
Text: New Baskerville

Very special thanks to:
Millie Barbee, Kate Barkschad, Ken
Botnick, Gary Clontz, John Cram, Dr.
Dinish Dave, Jan Davidson, Barbara
Duncan, Catherine Duncan, Mary
Cockrill, Jon Ellenbogen, Dr. Michael
Evans, David Goldhagen, Glen
Goodrich, Cheryl Hargrove, Steven
Heller, Jackie Holt, Betty Huskins,
Mary Jaeger-Gale, Jennifer Jenkins,
Bob Kopetsky, Jane Kristofferson,
Cindy Lennertz, Dan Miller, Catharine
Muerdter, Linda Morgan, Catherine
Morton, Harris Prevost, Dan Ray, Kirk
Schuly, Tim Shaw, Elizabeth Sims,
Tony Smith, Merrill Stebbins, Marla
Tambolini, Linda Taylor, Mark Taylor,
Melody Taylor, Jim Vedder, Nigel &
Kate Wilson.

Stay On Top Of The Trails
To get on our mailing list, call
1-800-331-4154. We'll keep you up to
speed about subsequent editions of
this book and trail updates. Use this
same number to order additional
guidebook copies for yourself, friends,
favorite aunts, and everyone in your
neighborhood.

Jay, Mark, Brad, Helen and Robin >

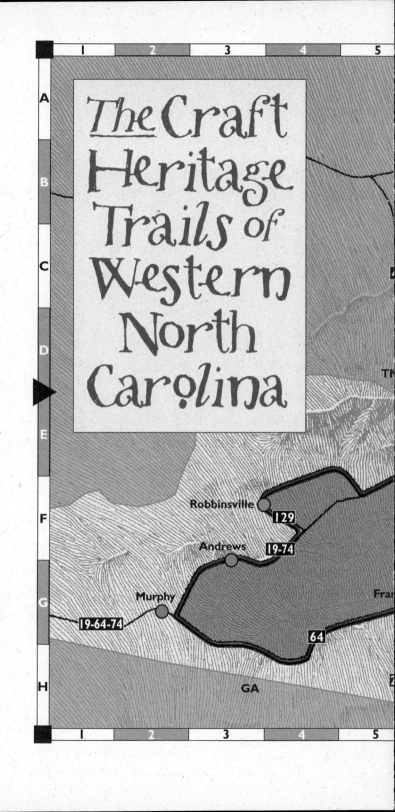

The Craft Heritage Trails of Western North Carolina

Robbinsville
129
Andrews
19-74
Murphy
19-64-74
64
Fra
TN
GA